www.davidsylvian.com

www.samadhisound.com

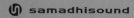 samadhisound

HYPERGRAPHIA

the writings of DAVID SYLVIAN

1980 - 2014

A WOUNDED DEER LEAPS HIGHEST

Emily Dickinson

It simply was what you did,
you didn't have a choice, even if
your words again and again were met
by silence, or those doors opened
to a world you couldn't abide.

from the house on the hill
_____

Stephen Dunn

This book is dedicated to my daughters
Ameera-Daya and Isobel Ananda

And to Richard Chadwick who made the implausible a reality

CONTENTS

Well it's been a long time

2/

1983 - 1984

If heaven watches over me

83/84 - BRILLIANT TREES   STEP 2

3/

1985 - 1986

In dresses white, all set for sail

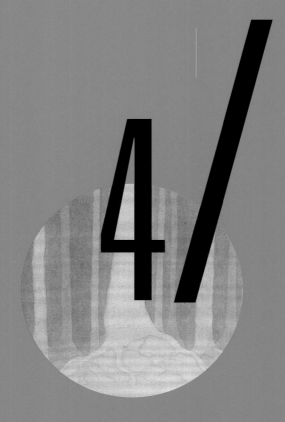

4/

1987 - 1988

Sipping coke and playing games

87/88 - SECRETS OF THE BEEHIVE   STEP 4

5/

1989 - 1991

We'd listen to the radio

89/91 - RAIN TREE CROW   STEP 5

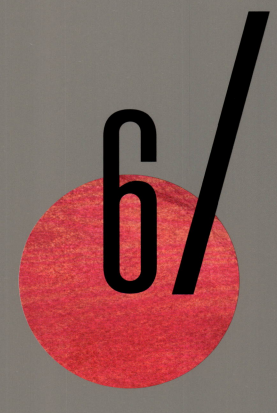

6/

1992 - 1993

And hurting

92/93 - THE FIRST DAY   STEP 6

1992 - 1993

My mother cries beneath a southern sky and I surrender

92/93 - DEAD BEES ON A CAKE   STEP 7

8/

2003 - 2005

She's forgotten I know

03/05 - BLEMISH   STEP 8

2003 - 2006

It's a wonderful world

03/06 - SNOW BORNE SORROW   STEP 9

2007 - 2014

Until the end of time

E S S A Y S

•

SYLVIANBOMB

by KEITH ROWE

pg. 41

WITNESS AND PARTICIPANT

a conversation with DAVID SYLVIAN

by NATALIA KUTSEPOVA

pg. 487

A CONVERSATION
ON THE SUBJECT OF MANAFON

an exchange between

DAVID SYLVIAN & MARCUS BOON

pg. 617

•

DAVID SYLVIAN

by KEITH ROWE

— **KR:** I can't resist wondering about the vision leading to "Manafon", an utterly unusual, rare piece of work. What led you to its conception? In the back of my mind is that widely reported conversation between Morton Feldman and Philip Guston in which Guston claims that he "does not finish a painting, but abandons it" instead, the point of abandonment occurring precisely "at the moment when it might become a painting." Guston desired to make rather than to make something. With "Manafon", was the impulse similar?

— **DS:** I'll offer the analogy of archaeology. Let's say that after decades of work you find yourself standing in a sunken pit facing a large, partially concealed doorway. The journey to reach this spot has been one of personal evolution and obsession. When you started out you had no idea this location existed. Over time, knowledge and potential deepen. Many issues you struggled with earlier on in life you now respond to intuitively. This intuitive expansion or broadening, a self seated squarely in the heart of the greater self, lays the groundwork for what must be done, leaves clues, tells you the where and the when of it, hints at the contents to be revealed. The more you rely on it, the more you come to trust in its wisdom even when it appears to lead you to points on a precipice. It beckons, you follow. Not blindly perhaps—although what is intuited is pre-verbal, the way forward is conveyed via a resonant network of signs and signals that you're equipped to interpret. So you find yourself before a door that will open onto an interior you feel you might recognise once you see it. You'll have to overcome numerous obstacles, but you'll navigate those as best you can until you're standing in the heart of the space. Once there, illuminated, the space is invigoratingly alive, immediate, tangible. It's utterly new to you, but it's also confirmation of what you had intuited: it's got a perceptible "thereness" about it. In those early sessions in Vienna we struck that particular kind of gold. I felt a sense of recognition and radical possibility. The evolution of my musical journey led me to that location accompanied by a team of experts in the field. An emotional excavation and a musical exploration in conjunction produced "Manafon", this odd genre-defying hybrid, a fairly unlikely meeting of two or more of music's diverse tributaries. The obvious reference point for me was the work I'd recently done with Derek Bailey for "Blemish"—it gave me a clue as to where this path of inquiry might lead. The working method I'd stumbled upon whilst recording that album had continued to prove itself more than up to the job of integrating original improv performances with lyrics and vocals. Expanding upon that one-on-one relationship with Derek to embrace larger improvising ensembles filled me with trepidation, but everyone involved, everyone, couldn't have been more gracious, which made the working experience relaxed, focused, and a real pleasure. An important part of the process was knowing the backgrounds of everyone involved, understanding the aesthetic at work, anticipating the chemistry of a particular constellation. This was the only "control" I could possibly exert prior to starting the process in motion. As for the Feldman/Guston quote, yes, the process is the important part of the journey, the making. But there's always a sense that it's a movement toward something, not necessarily the finished work, but onward. What happened with "Manafon"—which was a new experience for me—was that the work abandoned me. As I was writing and developing the material, the spirit holding all these disparate elements together just left me. I sat stunned for a moment and then realized: It's over; this is as far as it goes.

— **KR:** Your analogy of the pit and the door strikes a strong resonance within me. Being in the pit would be like attempting to comprehend the situation during a live performance. The door... never too sure about its construction. At times it seems made of 200 or more layers; other times it appears as if there are 200-plus separate doors, each one to be passed through. And now and again it's a kaleidoscope of apertures to be negotiated all at the same time. Each layer/door/aperture is an aspect of art or life that I should have considered before attempting to pass through, but there is no possibility of circumnavigation. I've started a list of these concerns that typically include affection, degrees of opacity, absorption, disclosure and withdrawal, illusions, the non-self, a phrase's architecture, the architecture of silence, harsh chimeras, anxiety, etc.
One aspect of negotiating these doors is that one is not alone. There seems to be a terracotta army of people around me. For instance, over my right shoulder is my old painting tutor Ben Hartley, on the other side is Cornelius Cardew, Gustav Mahler, Henry Purcell, Mark Rothko, Henri Poincaré, John Tilbury... .

— **DS:** Outside of the historical figures of the recent or distant past, I envy this notion of teachers and mentors. I felt their absence, particularly in my early years, when you'd likely be in most need of them. I stepped from a world of teenage self-absorption into an exploitative commercial world. By my own doing, of course, and it's the nature of that particular game, but there were no authority figures that didn't have a vested interest in a particular outcome, who weren't busy persuading me that I, in fact, desired the same outcome and approved of their methods. I've often wondered how different things would've been had I met just one truly insightful, financially un-invested individual during that period in time. Since that time I've obviously befriended peers with whom I felt it possible to absorb a fair amount via osmosis. Some artists, in whatever field, have an awful familiarity about them — it's like entering an asylum and looking into the eyes of the residents acknowledging that they too have seen what you've seen, are present but permanently otherwise engaged. In a sense it's a minority group which, like most minorities, by standing on the periphery by design or circumstance, is better equipped to see through the conformities of the societies to which we belong. This desire to belong, built into our DNA, is at odds with where we're likely to be at our most useful, our most functionally responsive. Although I've embraced a ghost-like community that aligns me with the work of artists of the past, it's healthy to reenact the process of separation at crucial periods to avoid stagnation or over-reliance. "Killing the father" — I feel I've been on something of a patricidal killing spree for the best part of the last decade.

— **KR:** Back to your observation on how new the situation leading to "Manafon" was for you. I would think that you would have needed to develop the necessary experiential hooks on which to hang the new experience. What in your past allowed you to recognise the significance of this new situation you found yourself in?

— **DS:** Since the early '80s I've been interested in deconstructing the familiar forms of popular song, in retaining the structure but removing the pillars of support. An underlying vein in my work continually returns to this question: How much of the framework can you remove whilst still being able to readily identify what is, after all, a very familiar form? Around 2001-02, I parted ways with Virgin Records after a long-term relationship that lasted some 21 years. A classical subsidiary of a major label that wanted to expand their horizons took an interest in me. Someone there put forward the suggestion that I take a look at the classical songbook, explore what already existed, and see if there wasn't a project that I might like to pursue. It wasn't such a bad idea so I did a little research, yet I came up empty-handed. There wasn't enough out there that offered an interesting formal challenge or that hadn't already been widely covered in one form or another. This got me thinking about alternate forms for popular song. What might I offer up to future generations for interpretation? Would it really have to be structurally more of the same? So I began a process of breaking things down, of embracing improvisation as a means of getting around my own limited ability to imagine new forms. With "Blemish" I started each day in the studio with a very simple improvisation on guitar. Once recorded, I'd listen back and use cues from the improv — the dynamic and so on — to dictate the structure of the piece. I'd write lyrics and melody on the spot, and then would follow that up with the recording of the vocal itself. Then I'd add a series of first takes, either on guitar or keyboards, and with a little editing everything fell into place quickly. I might have been skirting the issue of form, as the works themselves were often drone-based and open-ended, but it was a place for me to start. I kept this up for a few weeks, but then felt I needed a counterpoint to my own improvisations. I'd had Derek in the back of my mind at the outset of the project, so I gave him a call to see if he'd be interested in making a contribution that I might similarly respond to. He bemusedly questioned whether he was really the right person to do this. I said, "I'm looking for someone to present me with a challenge as a writer/vocalist." "In that case, I'm your man," he said. And so it started. I'd been listening to him since the '80s, so I could anticipate what might be coming my way, but had no idea how it was that I'd respond. He sent me about an hour's worth of solo material. I listened through once and singled out three pieces with which I thought I had a ghost of a chance and then approached them much as I did my own material. I wrote as I listened, a process of automatic writing if you will. Once the lyrics were in place, lined up melodically with precise moments in Derek's performance, I recorded on the spot. In a sense, I'd been steadily working my way toward "Manafon" since I was a young man listening to Stockhausen and dabbling in deconstructing the pop song. Having said that, I don't think we only develop as artists practicing in our chosen fields. For me that meant an exploration of intuitive states via meditation and other related disciplines which, the more I witnessed free-improv players at work, appeared to be crucially important to enable a being there in the present moment, a sustained alertness and receptivity.

— **KR:** Do you think that this process, in a sense, has a knock-on effect for those who have followed your music over the years? They find themselves in "Manafon", a new challenging situation; many may recognise its significance, while others—perhaps those without a mobility of attitude—find themselves at the door.

— **DS:** Without doubt. As lovers of popular music we have a consistent desire to relive that "shock of the new" experience we first had when young, but with a reluctance to embrace the shock element the second time around. There's that analogy of the man who was walking home late one evening when he looked up and was mesmerised by the unanticipated sight of a beautiful, bright, full moon in the sky. He resolves to come back the following evening to repeat the experience, but, of course, he can't because now he has expectations and the immediacy of the moment is lost. This is the dilemma for many listeners.

— **KR:** About those mentors who make up that terracotta army: they are utterly terrifying! For me they constitute a huge set of restrictions, emanating perhaps from a painting tutor screaming, "Rowe, only Caravaggio can paint Caravaggios!" I took this to mean I do not have permission to paint other people's painting, in profound contrast with music, where we do have permission to play other people's music.

— **DS:** I thought the army was there mainly to embolden, inspire, align... but walking in the footsteps of giants and self-censorship contribute to the evolution of one's true voice. With painting and drawing there is the problem of the empty canvas, which appears to have a particular silence that music has no hope of competing with: the artist's first mark seems to carry the weight of the past in a manner that is immediately apparent. The same with writing, of course. In a sense limitations are being circumnavigated by the range of sound embraced now as part of a musician's palette; it has increased fantastically over the last century or so, but, still, the issue is substance and the reconfiguration of the language itself, a re-ordering. With all that's at our disposal it shocks me that we don't hear more of what was once unimaginable. I'm not referring to the novelty of the new, but of something profoundly new that speaks with an authority capable of conveying a possibly transformative experience.

— **KR:** For me that would be the Cage/Tudor "Variations II" recording of 1961. When I first heard this in the mid- to late-'60s the shock, its significance, and its confirmation of what we were doing with AMM combined to make it one of the recordings I regard most highly. About the lack of an exact equivalent in music to the empty canvas: in the mid-'60s I simply regarded the electric guitar as an empty white canvas, an object to encounter, to stare at and imagine, What can I do with this thing? It helped to look at Cubist images of guitars and wonder how they would sound. My dissertation was on George Braque's guitars. The sense of liberation that emerged from detaching my grip on the instrument and abandoning its conventional technique was extraordinary. I directly applied the processes of the visual arts to this electric instrument: Pollock's when laying the guitar flat on its back and interacting with its surface; Duchamp's by using found objects such as knives, face fans, and cocktail mixers to play it; Rauschenberg's when integrating a radio. Regarding playing as painting offered, almost immediately, a new language for the instrument.

— **DS:** I know you've found yourself face to face with artists who have stolen directly from your palette and hung their works, so to speak, in the lobby of your own exhibition. It must be a difficult scenario to have to rise above. However, you found your voice long ago and it continues to mature with a confidence and a liberty to directly address the past. I'm thinking of the recent releases on Erstwhile ("ErstLive 007", Keith Rowe solo live at AMPLIFY 2008: light). Isn't this the difference between appropriation and an intuitive alignment or engagement, or confrontation, with the past?

— **KR:** I guess I'm firmly rooted in the past. I think we "absorb" and "move on" from the past rather than "reject" it. AMM was inspired by jazz, we learnt its essential lessons and then moved on to create a more relevant activity for us given our time and condition. But there are others whom I've engaged with as well: from Wagner we learned how to extend and stretch the material, from Mahler how to merge it, and from Rothko the process of oblique translation (from Michelangelo's Laurentian Library to the Seagram works). Hearing myself played back by someone else who has appropriated my own language at times is like looking in a mirror and realizing that somehow the nose is not quite right, the eyes are wrong, oh, and that hair! Where did that come from? Strange, but I don't mind. But you're right; such a language comes from a personal evolution and can't be short-circuited without a loss somewhere along the line.

— **DS:** You've said that back in the early days of AMM, you came to realise that you weren't black jazz musicians from Chicago, and therefore, although as listeners their idiom obviously spoke to you, you had to invent a language entirely your own. So you set about finding frameworks and strategies that allowed you to develop forms true to your own backgrounds. We've been through some radical changes in technological developments since and now the notion of community is far broader than it once was. We are able, and encouraged, to pull from a variety of sources that have less to do with geographical location than with aesthetic alignment. We're drawing our own cultural maps and possibly relocating to more suitable climates. Of course, we bring the baggage of who we are with us. Maybe what is gained by this rootless wandering (I tend to think of my generation as being the first to really do away with the notion of musical roots) is apparent, but, if you agree with any of the above, what, if anything, is lost in this development?

— **KR:** Your generation as the first to do away with musical roots? I'm not sure about this; I suspect this is a condition that many have felt throughout history, but, in a sense, the important aspect here maybe is not the issue of roots, but the possibility that no matter what we produce, no matter how radical we might think our new work is or how we feel it breaks with what has gone before, everything will, at some point, be absorbed into the mainstream. It's uncomfortable to realize that the improvisation from last week, in the fullness of history, can be placed right next to a Haydn string quartet! Scary thought, and a possible explanation for the overwhelming sense of failure many of us experience.

— **DS:** I should've prefaced that line by saying "the first generation of pop musicians," although your point still stands. We were the generation that experienced the melting pot of the '60s as kids, and as I'm sure you remember, '60s radio was in no way as segregated as it is today. We had to wade through every known form of popular music, from the ballads of previous generations, novelty hits, comedy turns, the brief history of rock and roll, Tin Pan Alley pop, reggae, soul, and so on, to hear the tracks that excited us at varying stages of our development. It was quite an education. Pop music being such an eclectic form, such a magpie, stealing from every source imaginable, this exposure to the broad scope of popular culture went on to create some interesting hybrids in the coming decades. I don't feel anchored or rooted in forms or disciplines that appear to be derived from a particular time and place, at least not in the sense that previous generations might've been, although this is all terribly subjective and possibly delusional. I'm at liberty to move across genres because, as a writer of song, none have a proprietary, cultural, or emotional hold on me over any other. The inevitability of absorption into the mainstream doesn't disturb me. To be this cell that reproduces over time and feeds into the cultural body is in some sense inevitable. I continue to describe myself as a pop musician because it's the least limiting of all definitions. Despite the fact that pop has started to recycle its past at an alarming rate, and its evolution continues, it is constantly redefining itself and could potentially embrace or absorb all manner of forms and ideas. In this respect "Manafon" is a pop album. You could replace my voice with voices of the past and it would take a small step into an alternate future Imagine Sinatra or Hartmann singing these songs! It takes just the smallest of leaps.

— **KR:** A short while after hearing "Manafon" for the first time I had a strong need and desire to place your voice, not in any sense to fix it, but to just get a grip of where it resides for me. There's a very fluid triangulation somewhere between Bryn Terfel's rendering of Handel's "Ombra Mai Fu", Esther Phillips's "And I Love Him", and "Adieu, Sweet Lovely Nancy" by The Copper Family of Rottingdean. What particularly strikes me in "Manafon" is how you combine two different worlds from the spectrum of music, which is difficult: I recall reading how the great George Cziffra found performing Chopin and Liszt in the same program difficult, since for him Chopin is the poet who speaks and Liszt is the great orator. The poet and the orator, a possible response to your voice in "Manafon".

— **DS:** I attempted to fuse two worlds. I say "two" but there are probably more at work. There's a world of difference between writing lyrics and writing poetry, but it's difficult to define what that difference is. Between the lines of a poem there's an entire universe, and between the lines of a lyric there's silence. Because the poem is complete in itself, performing the work with musical accompaniment, no matter how sensitive and accomplished this accompaniment might be, is redundant: decorative wallpaper on which to hang a Rothko. I attempted to create work that had the power of poetry, but which was designed and born out of the musical environment sustaining it. The audio accompaniment supplies the "universe," there's ample room for both it and the lyrics to play crucial roles in the total composition. An absence of redundant emphasis and echoes — that was the goal anyway. The models were spoken word, chamber music, and chamber theatre. Maybe the latter was the more important in that you have a central

narrator conveying the narrative, but, because of the intimate and possibly spare nature of the presentation, every aspect of the stage design and direction becomes essential in enhancing the nuance expressed by the central voice. That's not even beginning to tackle the melodic content of the compositions themselves, which reference folk, jazz, pop, musical theatre, and more. This was the luxury of working with material that suggested much, but which remained open, mercurial. It afforded me liberty both as melodist and lyricist. Melodically, I responded naturally, moving fluidly from one reference to another in the original improvisations as I heard them. Lyrically, I was able to use language in a rather prosaic, everyday manner where appropriate, or switch to a more refined vocabulary that could've sounded terribly precious outside of this context. The environment was very forgiving, embracing everything I threw at it. The subject of my voice is difficult for me to get into; it's far too subjective. I can only comment on the technical aspect of trying to address the mode or degree of performance in just about every other line written: How much emphasis to place here? Should this line be spoken as much as sung? Should it be dismissive, playful, internalized, self-pitiful, or sung simply, beautifully?

— **KR:** Matisse, Haydn, Picasso, Elliott Carter, Leonardo, Merce Cunningham, John Cage, to name but a few, are artists whose work had an exceptional consistency, and who managed to remain creative throughout their lives. Other than Derek Bailey it's difficult to think of any of all those young, radical guitar players hanging around London in the '60s who retained their adventurous investigations beyond their early thirties. Making challenging work, to me anyhow, does not appear to be what their lives have been about, whereas "Manafon" is a real challenge!

— **DS:** Thank you. I'm not sure I can claim consistency, but then again, life is anything but. Horses for courses. I don't doubt that many of the lastingly popular artists of our time have a similar commitment to the work, but the emphasis is placed elsewhere. We're talking comfort zones, priorities, and lifestyles, aren't we? A challenge embodies the risk of failure, and with age it's possible that many artists don't want to risk losing face. It's necessary to dare to be risible to some degree. This comes easier to youth in its naivety and bravado than to older generations, perhaps? But then again, I doubt anyone would wish for an exclusive diet of the challengingly new, as there's plenty of great work out there to be absorbed and digested. What we don't tend to have enough of is an approach to popular music that does to form what extended technique does for the evolution of the instruments themselves. How many generations has it taken for a man who came at the guitar from such a unique perspective as yours, referencing aerial bombardment, modern art, and the cubist guitars of George Braque to wind up contributing to the possible evolution of popular song?

— **KR:** Gosh! The notion that I might make even the slightest contribution to a possible evolution to the popular song seems such an unlikely thought to me. I say this because I've struggled throughout my entire life to find anything of interest within pop music. I'd need in haste to draw a distinction between pop and popular music—in the latter there is a reasonable amount I listen to (Mercedes Sosa, John Lee Hooker, Ali Farka Touré, Abed Azrié, Astor Piazzolla, Junior Brown), but the shelves are almost bare in the pop cupboard, with the possible exceptions of The Beach Boys' "Don't Talk (Put Your Head on my Shoulder)", and the aforementioned Esther Phillips.

— **DS:** I meant evolution in popular song in the broadest sense, or in some alternate universe. Pop embraces so many influences and possible offshoots: John Lee Hooker as absorbed into the body of Tom Waits, Ali Farka Touré into the body of Paul Simon, which, in turn, feeds the hunger of younger generations digesting the influence further, such as Vampire Weekend. I'm no musicologist, but you can hear these strains of influence enter into the mainstream in a myriad of forms. I'm certain this will increasingly prove to be the case as shared community experiences break down further over time. No longer network TV or broadcast radio with which we might share a common experience or exposure. It would appear to be a case of personal discriminatory listening tapping into the multiplicity of sources available to us. Everything's available all at once. In that sense at least all is contemporaneous.

— **KR:** My inability to locate any significance in 98 percent of popular culture seems like an affliction. I'm never sure how this suchness was arrived at: was it the five years of training in fine art, or hardwiring? What I do know is that having my nose so very close to my own canvas, monitoring each and every move, unrelentingly severe, results in a hardboiled stance that has survived without a caring public.

— **DS:** We come back to process. It's a lifetime's journey, a personal evolution. Instinct and awareness finely-tuned, necessary blind spots in place to avoid the pitfall of being seduced by other concerns. I've allowed myself to be frequently sidetracked in life and work. For the most part, something positive has arisen out of most circumstances in one form or another, but as I get older, I'm less inclined to enter into partnerships that deviate from a certain course I've set for myself. Sound is seductive, though. Sometimes you're seduced before you've had time to put up a decent resistance. Yet given the option, I'm not sure I'd have it any other way. Still you don't use all the tools in the toolbox just because they're at hand. Using your discrimination, you take from the world and the work of others whatever resonates and bring it to the table in an effort to substantiate your own sense of purpose or practice. To inform and bolster your own interior world, no? I personally find I need less input from a cultural perspective. I've found physical isolation beneficial in this respect. Are you somewhat culturally isolated in your home in France?

— **KR:** Isolation? Here in the vineyards of western France, yes, totally, but I don't mind that. I recall Cardew talking about the avoidance of being a big fish in a small pond... here, culturally, it's no fish in a small, very small pond. And the future? What might this hold for you?

— **DS:** A reordering is on the cards. I've been working on and off with contemporary classical composer Dai Fujikura. He's already started reworking elements of "Manafon" further confusing its genealogy. This may result in what we're currently referring to as a re-imagined version of the album with additional material. We've also written new material unassociated with this project and are looking to see how we might build upon it. Again, uncharted territory for me. To counter this I've been sitting with an old semi-acoustic Gibson enjoying the simplicity of writing miniatures. If there are goals in mind they're not fully formed. A temporary lapse into silence has been necessary so as to hear what comes next, if anything.

— **KR:** I look forward to hearing how a re-imagined version of "Manafon" sounds. I'm attracted to that phrase, and Gerald M. Edelman's remembered present: "Every act of perception to some degree is an act of creation, and every act of memory is to some degree an act of imagination."

— **DS:** Yes, I think it was Cocteau that said you must be inspired to read. We could keep trading quotations for days. The notion of the audience's engagement with a performance as an intrinsically passive act has never been something I've bought into. Both as performer and viewer I've felt the importance of the audience's role in a shared, participatory awareness. It definitely has the potential to up the ante in terms of what might be achieved on a given night. I've found that most performers are generally acutely aware of this. Some psychoanalysts talk about the narratives of our lives... that when our narratives hit some sort of pothole and we're unable to reconcile the internal narrative with external events say, we hit crisis. We need help re-writing the narrative to allow for current developments, to help us make sense of things. This suggests that our waking lives are a form of storytelling, are a creative act. As someone kindly reminded me recently, you are the author of your life. How about you? Where do you find yourself at present?

— **KR:** I'm just now preparing my setup for the year's first performance in Kitakyushu, Japan. I continue with a finger trainer influenced by Lorenzo Lotto as the main performance instrument. Stay patient as the airport security queue gets longer and longer.

— **DS:** Ah, in transit and in-security! The psychological life of the artist. Life for me has been a little bit like checking into a hotel, sleeping fully dressed on top of the bed covers, bags still packed, in anticipation of departure the following morning. I'm not advocating this approach. It's just an observation. ... As a footnote, Cage on the subject of beauty:

"The first question I ask myself when something doesn't seem to be beautiful, the first question I ask is why do I think it's not beautiful? And very shortly you discover there is no reason."

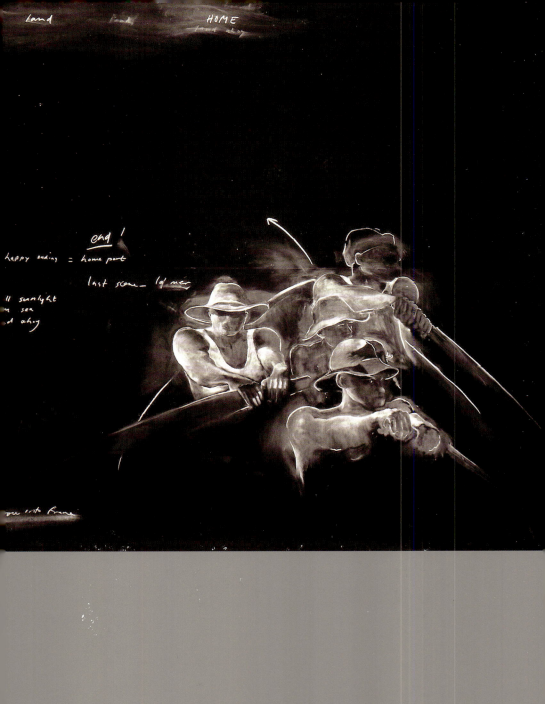

Land   HOME

end !

happy ending = home port

      last scene – la' mer

sunlight
sea
ahoy

A

S Y L V I A N

S T E P

1

THE OTHER SIDE OF LIFE

Well it's been a long time
How should I feel
What can I say?

With fantastic stories
You present yourself
In different ways

Some particular places
Remembered so well
Are hard to forget

We've travelled so far now
Then we were young
Hard to impress

But she comes and goes
The other side of life
Sheltering only the other side of life

These single occasions
We seem to share
Stumble and fall

If you could remember to wave
A sign of life my way

But she comes and goes
The other side of life
Sheltering only the other side of life

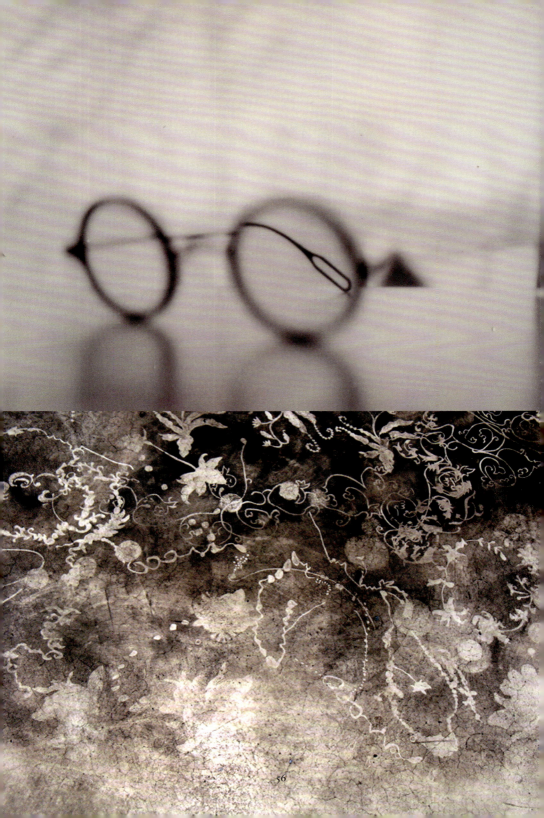

SOME KIND OF FOOL

Maybe I'm wrong
I should just keep moving on
I suppose
But I'll see it through just like some kind of fool

You say you care
But this kind of life leads nowhere
Still I guess
I'll see it through just like some kind of fool

The rules of the game
We constantly play can be cruel
If nothing else remains
I've promised to stay
And I do

Crying again
You say these words are just sentimental things
But I'll stay with you just like some kind of fool

All the things we say
Apportioning blame
Are untrue
Though nothing else remains
I've promised to stay
And I do
And I do
Like some kind of fool

The rules of the game
We so often play can be cruel
If nothing else remains
I've promised to stay
And I do
And I do
Like some kind of fool

NIGHTPORTER

Could I ever explain
This feeling of love that just lingers on
This fear in my heart
That keeps telling me which way to turn?

We'll wander again
Our clothes they are wet
We shy from the rain
Longing to touch all the places we know we can hide
The width of a room
That could hold so much pleasure inside

Here am I alone again
A quiet town where life gives in
Here am I just wondering
Nightporters go
Nightporters slip away

I'll watch for a sign
And if I should ever again cross your mind
I'll sit in my room and wait until night life begins
Then catching my breath we'll both brave the weather
again

Here am I alone again
A quiet town where life gives in
Here am I just wondering
Nightporters go
Nightporters slip away

GHOSTS

When the room is quiet
The daylight almost gone
It seems there's something I should know

Well I ought to leave
But the rain it never stops
And I've no particular place to go

Just when I think I'm winning
When I've broken every door
The ghosts of my life
Blow wilder than before
Just when I thought I could not be stopped
When my chance came to be king
The ghosts of my life blew wilder than the wind

Well I'm feeling nervous
Now I find myself alone
The simple life's no longer there
Once I was so sure
Now the doubt inside my mind
Comes and goes but leads nowhere

Just when I think I'm winning
When I've broken every door
The ghosts of my life
Blow wilder than before
Just when I thought I could not be stopped
When my chance came to be king
The ghosts of my life blew wilder than the wind

FORBIDDEN COLOURS

The wounds on your hands never seem to heal
I thought all I needed was to believe

Here am I, a lifetime away from you
The blood of Christ, or the beat of my heart
My love wears forbidden colours
My life believes

Senseless years thunder by
Millions are willing to give their lives for you
Does nothing live on?

Learning to cope with feelings aroused in me
My hands in the soil, buried inside of myself
My love wears forbidden colours
My life believes in you once again

I'll go walking in circles
While doubting the very ground beneath me
Trying to show unquestioning faith in everything
Here am I, a lifetime away from you
The blood of Christ, or a change of heart

My love wears forbidden colours
My life believes
My love wears forbidden colours
My life believes in you once again

BAMBOO HOUSES

All the buildings I have loved
Are barely standing
All the children, too young and thin
Sing bamboo music

BAMBOO MUSIC

I walk through open fields
Where children sing
Bamboo music

A song of life itself
Played to win
In bamboo music

(We work)
Working harder still
(Down where life begins)
From here to heaven

(We fight)
Fighting harder still
(Down where life begins)
From here to heaven

Building bamboo houses by the million
Lighting fires that only burn inside
Singing bamboo music by the million
Fighting for our lives

I walk through open fields
Where children sing
Bamboo music

A song of life itself
Of sun and steel
In bamboo music

83/84 - BRILLIANT TREES

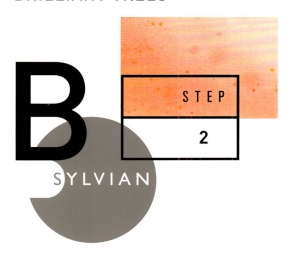

B

SYLVIAN

STEP

2

BRILLIANT TREES

david sylvian brilliant trees

←——— WIND

Storm up ①

SH

PULLING PUNCHES

If heaven watches over me
Sowing seeds back in the soil
With eyes that see, hands that feel
Why am I the last to know?

Sheltered lives spent partially breathing
Are gathered together under new religion
Pulling punches, sleeping on our feet
Pulling punches, I needed someone to comfort me

Raised in summer days of splendour
Who would've dreamed of love never ending

A better world lies in front of me
A sketch of life in the books I read
Then as I walk where heaven leads
Why am I the last to know?

Simple lives spent partially breathing
Are gathered together under new religion

Pulling punches, sleeping on our feet
Pulling punches, I needed someone to comfort me
Raised in summer days of splendour
Who would've dreamed of love never ending

Nature feeds this nausea
Deep inside the heart of me

Sheltered lives spent partially breathing
Are gathered together under new religion

THE INK IN THE WELL

The lights of the ashes smoulder through hills and vales
Nostalgia burns in the hearts of the strongest
Picasso is painting the ships in the harbour
The wind and sails
These are years with a genius for living

The rope is cut, the rabbit is loose
(Fire at will in this open season)
The blood of a poet, the ink in the well
(It's all written down in this age of reason)

The animals run through harvested fields of fire
The bitterness shown on the face of the homeless
Picasso is painting the flames from the houses
The sudden rain
These are years with a genius for living

The rope has been cut, the rabbit is loose
(Fire at will in this open season)
The blood of a poet, the ink in the well
(It's all written down in this age of reason)

Fire at will

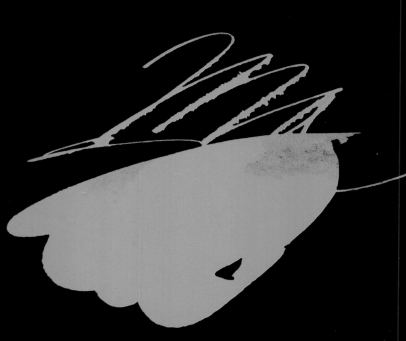

NOSTALGIA

Voices heard in fields of green
Their joy their calm and luxury
Are lost within the wanderings of my mind
I'm cutting branches from the trees
Shaped by years of memories
To exorcise their ghosts from inside of me

The sound of waves in a pool of water
I'm drowning in my nostalgia

RED GUITAR

I recognise no method of living that I know
I see only the basic materials I may use

If you ask me, I may tell you
It's been this way for years

I play my red guitar
It's the devil in the flesh
It's the iron in my soul

I understand you're facing problems inside you
A certain difficulty of being that I know too

You may ask me why do I fail
Just when I'm needed?

I play my red guitar
It's the devil in the flesh
It's the iron in my soul

If you ask me, I may tell you
It's been this way for years

WEATHERED WALL

You were someone to believe in
A place for hope in a changing world
Feeling every moment
Every one of the years spent in your arms

After a lifetime of living
These soiled hands show no life at all
Working at all hours
Never facing the fears here in my heart

Grieving for the loss of heaven
Weeping for the loss of heaven
By the wailing wall

You were someone to believe in
Giving life where there was a will to learn
But it's the nature of living
To count only the years left in your heart

Grieving for the loss of heaven
Weeping for the loss of heaven
By the wailing wall

BACKWATERS

Once again I'm hiding in backwaters
Running this way and that
Trying so very hard to please

(Beware of hidden snares)

Rushing to bite the hand that feeds me
Running this way and that

(There are always other possibilities)

This way and that

BRILLIANT TREES

When you come to me
I'll question myself again
Is this grip on life still my own

When every step I take
Leads me so far away
Every thought should bring me closer home

And there you stand
Making my life possible
Raise my hands up to heaven
But only you could know

My whole world stands in front of me
By the look in your eyes
By the look in your eyes
My whole life stretches in front of me
Reaching up like a flower
Leading my life back to the soil

Every plan I've made's
Lost in the scheme of things
Within each lesson lies the price to learn

A reason to believe
Divorces itself from me
Every hope I hold lies in my arms

And there you stand
Making my life possible
Raise my hands up to heaven
But only you could know

My whole world stands in front of me
By the look in your eyes
By the look in your eyes
My whole life stretches in front of me
Reaching up like a flower
Leading my life back to the soil

NAGARKOT

BEYOND ALL DOUBT THERE IS A PLACE
THAT PLACE
VAST RIVERS, TALL MOUNTAINS
TINY BOATS
SOME OLD AND FORGOTTEN
SOME MAKING THEIR WAY FOR THE VERY FIRST TIME
ACROSS THE MISCHIEVOUS RIPPLES OF THE YAWNING DEEP
I STAND QUIETLY ON A HILLTOP (NAGARKOT)
WAITING FOR STILLNESS
CALM
THAT I TOO MAY MAKE THE JOURNEY
THAT LONG AND PERILOUS JOURNEY
HARD NAILS, OAK WOOD
AND A HEAVY HEART
HOME

Words With The Shaman

Preparations for a Journey

CAUTION
踏切注意

Steel Cathedrals

85/86 - GONE TO EARTH

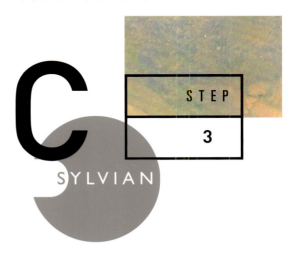

C

SYLVIAN

STEP

3

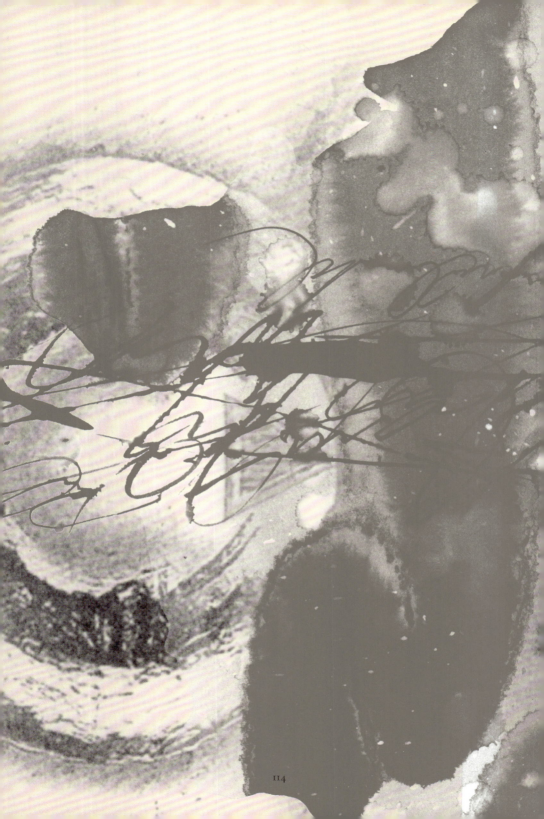

GONE TO EARTH

TAKING THE VEIL

In dresses white, all set for sail
A little girl dreams of taking the veil

In dresses white, all set for sail
A little girl dreams of taking the veil
On beaches clean of sand and shell
A little girl dreams of taking the veil

All lightning bright and thunder loud
A little girl dreams safe and sound

LAUGHTER AND FORGETTING

Running like a horse between the trees
The ground beneath my feet
Gives me something to hold onto

With the reins around my heart
Guided by hands that spread life before my very eyes

Well every hope falls down on its knees in time
But I'm no longer lost
Every day, every second, every hour inside
Love's my only guide

Are these the years for laughter and forgetting?

BEFORE THE BULLFIGHT

I hear your voice
Way down inside
A whispering sea of towering trees
But no reply

A silence so rare
And more than I can stand
Sweeps like a flood through life's flesh and blood
And steals away with its heart

If I'm losing you
Then there's nothing more that I can say
The fighting is on and battles are won
Or thrown away

But if I could live
Safe and sound
In God-given fields or mountains of steel
Then here I'd stay 'til you'd gone

Guilty of stealing every thought I own
I will take my turn to fight the bullfight
Every word's sunk in deep
Like the blades of a knife through my heart
But my strength will return
To fight the bullfight

As time's come to show
I'm told nothing more than I should know
A ship on the sea that threatens to leave
But never goes

This island of blue
Where life clings to your hands
Like water and sand
Will lose its way when you're gone

When all's forgiven
Still every fault's my own
I will take my turn to fight the bullfight
Say a prayer for my release
When every hope in the world is asleep
And my strength will return
To fight the bullfight

GONE TO EARTH

With a burning candle
A book of holy things
They'll throw you up against the wall
Bind your hands with string
Caught in this sudden shower
Our host of heavenly kings
They're all victims of circumstance
Of ancient bells that bring
All the fear in the world, naked and shy
Down upon our heads with no reason why

And though voices may holler
For all they're worth
The rabbits have fled their burrows
Gone to earth

WAVE

It seems that I remember I dreamed a thousand dreams
We'd face the days together no matter what they'd bring
A strength inside like I'd never known
Opened the door to life and let it go

This sun may shine forever upon the back of love
A kingdom raised from ashes and held within your arms
And should the rain break through the trees
We'll find a shelter there and never leave

I'll run to you
Nothing stands between us now
Nothing I can lose
This light inside can never die
Another world just made for two
I'll swim the seas inside with you
And like the waves without a sound
I'll never let you down

Upon a wave of summer
A hilltop paved with gold
We shut our eyes and made the promises we hold
A will to guide and see us through
I'd do it all again because of you

I'll run to you
Nothing stands between us now
Nothing I can lose
This light inside can never die
Another world just made for two
I'll swim the seas inside with you
And like the waves without a sound
I'll never let you down

I'd tear my very soul to make you mine

RIVERMAN

I see your eyes light up like fire
It's medicine to me
But as the hunted live their lives
You're keeping out of reach

So I keep running, falling
'Til I reach the water
Run with me holyman
But when I reach out
I find I'm standing right beside her
Now we're living
Blessed with all the thunder in the world

Now should you ask me to come home
To wake up from the sleep
Like a boat inside a storm
Is there no hope for me?

So I keep running, falling
Wade into the water
Run with me riverman
But when I reach out
I find I'm standing right beside her
Now we're living
Blessed with all the thunder in the world

SILVER MOON

Out upon the open fields
The rain is pouring down
We're pulling up the sheets again
Against the passing tides of love
Every doubt that holds you here
Will find its own way out

I will build a shelter if you call
Just take my hand and walk
Over mountains high and wide
Bridging rivers deep inside
With a will to guide you on
Your heart will need no one
Those days are gone

Baby I can tell you there's no easy way out
Lost inside of dreams that guide you on
Baby I can tell you there's no easy way out
Soon the guiding moonlight will be gone

Out upon the ocean waves subside
From the weakness of the tide
That punishes in kind
When the heavens open wide
Every shore the moon shines on
Every word her sirens sung
"Believe in no one"

Baby I can tell you there's no easy way out
Lost inside of dreams that guide you on
Baby I can tell you there's no easy way out
Soon the guiding moonlight will be gone

A BIRD OF PREY VANISHES INTO A DEEP BLUE CLOUDLESS SKY

THE HEALING PLACE

ANSWERED PRAYERS

WHERE THE RAILROAD MEETS THE SEA

THE WOODEN CROSS

SILVER MOON OVER SLEEPING STEEPLES

CAMP FIRE: COYOTE COUNTRY

HOME

SUNLIGHT SEEN THROUGH TOWERING TREES

UPON THIS EARTH

THE COLOUR OF ROSES

The thoughts of many men
Came by word of mouth
And burnt like a thorn in my side
They parted with the book
I parted with the cash
And I rolled the pages over

And wisdom just fell into my hands

Now my heart bleeds the colour of roses

I'm a cactus in the sand
A mountain goat
Firmly holding my ground
I'm fighting in the dark
The compass and the kings
Wearing infinity's armour

And the weapons just fell into my hands

Now my heart bleeds the colour of roses

In the darkness of the wood
Where the witches, one by one
Burn their offerings to the moon
I close my eyes

LILITH

The house is quiet and still
Set in a valley of green
She walks in the shade of the hills
And charms the birds from the trees
Silencing questions in me

She sings in my brightest of dreams
The songs of shaman and kings
With a voice that could tear through the clouds
In the sky

See us rise on a will to power
While others still sleep
A forest in full flower
Where every river runs deep
The holy blood of saints and sheep

BUOY

Underneath a burning sun
There's always work to be done
We take much more than we care to give away

You'll be the moth, I'm the flame
I'll bless you and keep you safe and sound until
Sunrise comes around again

I'm like a mountain made of stone
I'm like a new day dawning
I'll be here every morning, close to you

We'll sail on a river, way out to the Baltic sea
Love will keep us together
And the tide will draw you close to me
(Never words so true, never words so wise)
Love will keep us together
'Cause there's more to this than meets the eye

I burn a candle in your place
I picture the passions on your face
Feelings that rise on a wave and fall away

All the pleasures have returned
All of the lessons I should have learned
Return again to light, for us to see

You're like a map of buried gold
I search for treasures in your soul
And when I'm gone you'll know I will come back to you

We'll sail on a river, way down to the salty sea
Love will keep us together
And the tide will draw you close to me
(Never words so true, never words so wise)
Love will keep us together
'Cause there's more to this than meets the eye

I'm like a mountain, made of stone
I'm like a new day dawning
i'll be here every morning, close to you

87/88 - SECRETS OF THE BEEHIVE

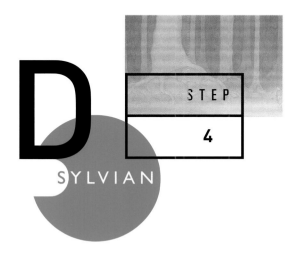

D

SYLVIAN

STEP

4

147

SECRETS OF THE BEEHIVE

DAVID SY

Secrets of th

SEPTEMBER

The sun shines high above the sounds of laughter
The birds swoop down upon the crosses of old grey churches
We say that we're in love while secretly wishing for rain
Sipping coke and playing games

September's here again
September's here again

THE BOY WITH THE GUN

He knows well his wicked ways
A course of bitterness
A grudge held from his childhood days
As if life had loved him less
Reading down his list of names
He ticks them one by one
He points the barrel at the sky
Firing shots off at the sun

"I am the law and I am the king
I am the wisdom, listen to me sing"

He carves out the victims' names
In the wooden butt of the gun
He leans well back against the tree
He knows his kingdom's come
He breathes a sigh self satisfied
The work is in good hands
He shoots the coins into the air
And follows where the money lands

"I am the law and I am the king
I am the wisdom, listen to me sing"

He pauses at the city's edge
Of hellfire and of stone
He summons up the devil there
To give him courage of his own
He'll free the sinners of deceit
They'll hear his name and run
His justice is his own reward
Measured out beneath the sun

"I am the law and I am the king
I am the wisdom, listen to me sing"

And my name's on the gun

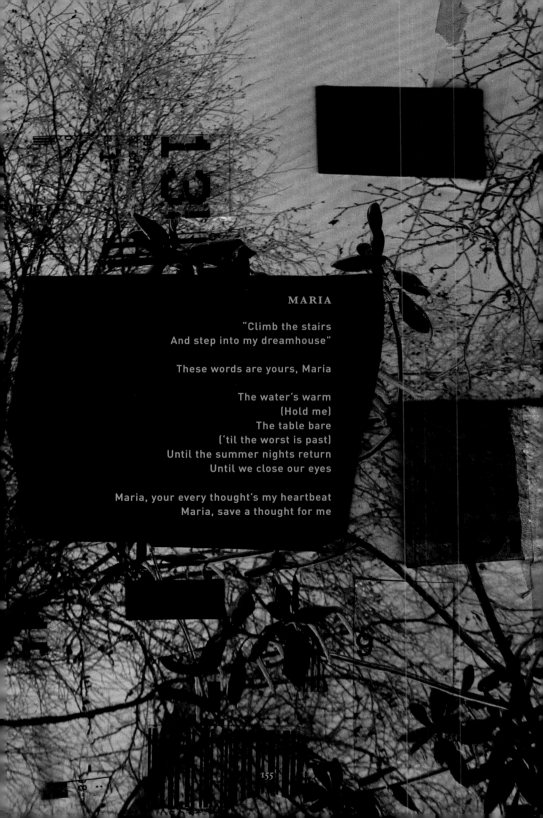

MARIA

"Climb the stairs
And step into my dreamhouse"

These words are yours, Maria

The water's warm
(Hold me)
The table bare
('til the worst is past)
Until the summer nights return
Until we close our eyes

Maria, your every thought's my heartbeat
Maria, save a thought for me

rain

157

ORPHEUS

Standing firm on this stony ground
The wind blows hard
Pulls these clothes around
I harbour all the same worries as most
The temptation's to leave or to give up the ghost
I wrestle with an outlook on life
That shifts between darkness and shadowy light
I struggle with words for fear that they'll hear
But Orpheus sleeps on his back still dead to the world

Sunlight falls, my wings open wide
There's a beauty here I cannot deny
And bottles that tumble and crash on the stairs
Are just so many people I knew never cared
Down below on the wreck of the ship
Are a stronghold of pleasures I couldn't regret
But the baggage is swallowed up by the tide
As Orpheus keeps to his promise and stays by my side

Tell me, I've still a lot to learn
Understand, these fires never stop
Believe me, when this joke is tired of laughing
I will hear the promise of my Orpheus sing

Sleepers sleep as we row the boat
Just you the weather and I gave up hope
But all of the hurdles that fell in our laps
Were fuel for the fire and straw for our backs
Still the voices have stories to tell
Of the power struggles in heaven and hell
But we feel secure against such mighty dreams
As Orpheus sings of the promise tomorrow may bring

Tell me, I've still a lot to learn
Understand, these fires never stop
Please believe, when this joke is tired of laughing
I will hear the promise of my Orpheus sing

THE DEVIL'S OWN

The night is dark and cold
The strong winds and the rain
Crack the branches upon my window
The devil beats his drum
Casting out his spell
Dragging all his own down into hell

The ticking of the clock
Inexorably goes on
The howling of the stray souls of heaven
The treasures of the cove
Where the traders stored their gold
Echo voices still dead to the world

Underneath the vine
Shaded by the leaves
I still hold you close to me
Beneath the open stars
Beneath the pillows and the sheets
I still hold you dear to me

The ticking of the clock
Surely sunrise won't be long
When darkness hides inside its own shadow
The devil beats his drum
Casting out his name
Dragging all his own down into shame

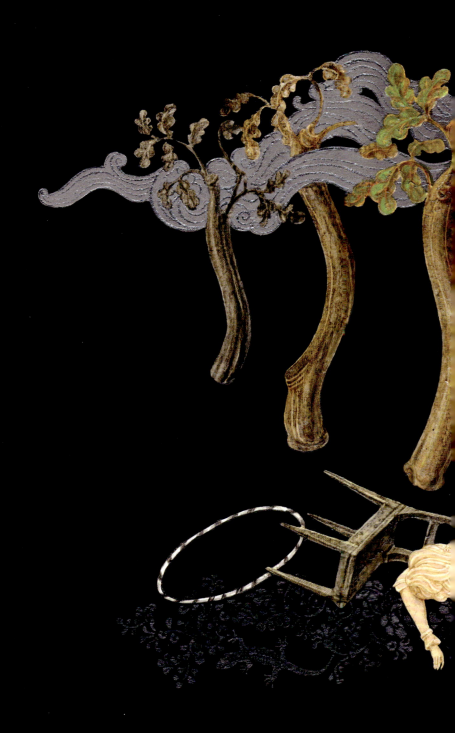

WHEN POETS DREAMED OF ANGELS

She rises early from bed
Runs to the mirror
The bruises inflicted in moments of fury

He kneels beside her once more
Whispers a promise
"Next time I'll break every bone in your body"

And wellwishers let the devil in
nd if the river ran dry they'd deny it happening

As the cardplayers deal their hands
From the bottom of the deck

Row upon row of feudal houses blow away
Medicine for the popular complaint

When the poets dreamed of angels
What did they see?
History lined up in a flash at their backs

When the poets dreamed of angels
What did they see?
The bishops and knights
well placed to attack

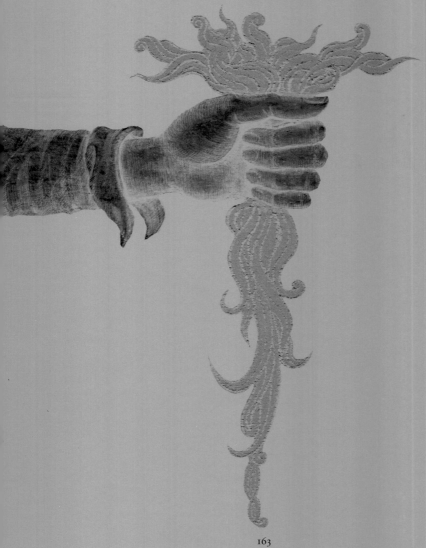

163

MOTHER AND CHILD

Shadows form knights and pawns
Upon the squares
Blood is drawn up from the well
Secret signs brought the crime
Right to your door
An innocent guilty as hell

Oh the cot is open wide
Damp with milk and honey
Gone the mother and the child
In Jesus' name

Should they be waiting there
On my return
I may run into their arms
Walking on a razor's edge
Unconcerned
Game is lost again
I'll never learn

LET THE HAPPINESS IN

I'm waiting on the empty docks
Watching the ships come in
I'm waiting for the agony to stop
Oh let the happiness in

I'm watching as the gulls all settle down
Upon the empty vessels
The faded whites of their wedding gowns
The song of hopeless selflessness

The cold December sun
A cold that blisters
The hands of a working man
Wasted

I'm waiting on the empty docks
Watching the ships roll in
I'm longing for the agony to stop
Oh let the happiness in

Oh let the happiness in

Listen to the waves against the rocks
I don't know where they've been
I'm waiting for the sky to open up
And let the happiness in

Oh let the happiness in

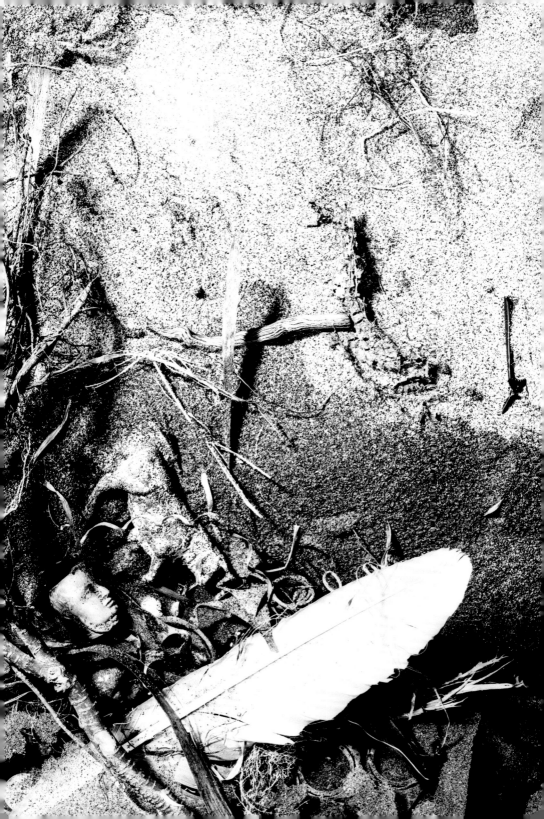

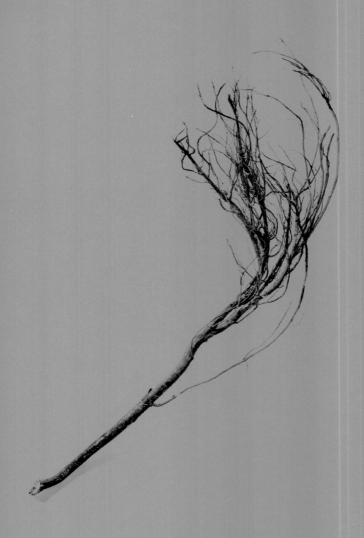

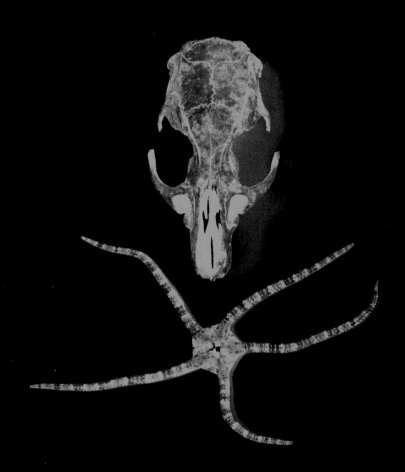

WATERFRONT

On the banks of a sunset beach
Messages scratched in sand
Beneath a roaming home of stars
Young boys try their hand
A Spanish harbouring of sorts
In Catalonian bars
They were pulled from a sinking ship
And saved for last

On the waterfront the rain
Is pouring in my heart
Here the memories come in waves
Raking in the lost and found of years
And though I'd like to laugh
At all the things that led me on
Somehow the stigma still remains

Watch the train steam full ahead
As it takes the bend
Empty carriages lose their tracks
And tumble to their end

So the world shrinks drop by drop
As the wine goes to your head
Swollen angels point and laugh
"This time your God is dead"

On the waterfront the rain
Is pouring in my heart
Here the memories come in waves
Raking in the lost and found of years
And though I'd like to laugh
At all the things that led me on
Somehow the stigma still remains

Is our love strong enough?

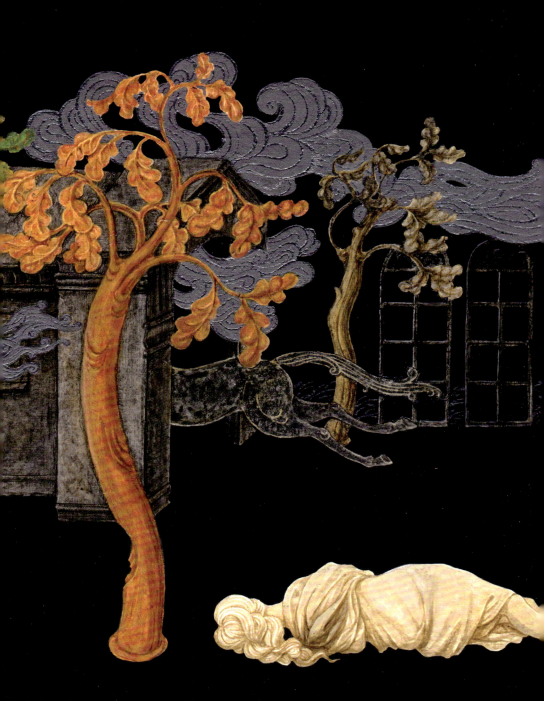

174

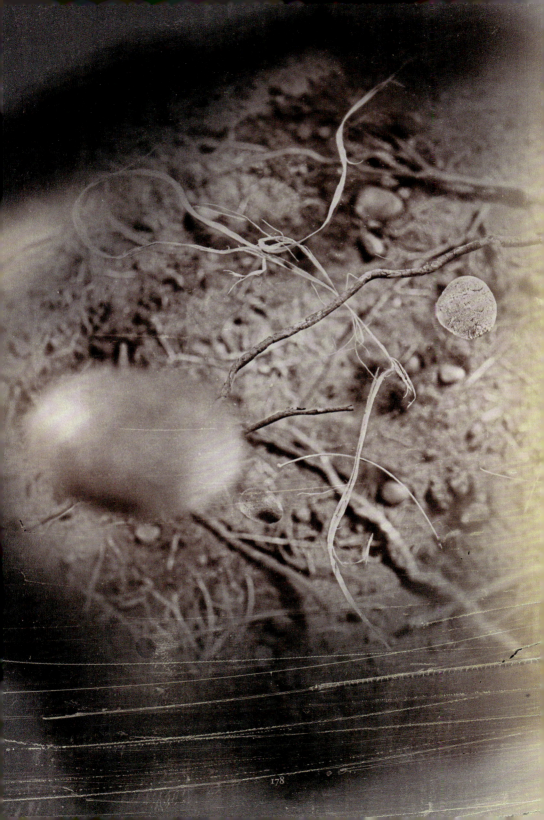

PROMISE (THE CULT OF EURYDICE)

The silence of the park
The moonshine after dark
Came to keep her company
The tiny golden cross
Lay upon her throat
Hands clutching tight her rosary

The rain upon her lips
Eyes opened with a kiss
Just too late for us to see
She sits upon the ground
Face covered by a shroud
Of midnight canopy

And when the lightning starts
The secrets in her heart
Merge within the rain patterns
And when the shadows fall
The promise of it all
Is lost inside the tears that linger on

All the things we'd hoped
Would always keep us close
Stand between us now as fences
The letters that we wrote
Have all gone up in smoke
And now you're just too far to listen in

When all but hope is lost
You believe at any cost
In things that make the living lighter
And when the shadows fall
The promise of it all
Is lying in the bed beside her

RIDE

Messages ran all over town
Words without sound
Condemned me
And left me for dead
All over again
It wasn't the first time, but this time
Things will never be the same

Ride
Ride the very thought into the ground
In the church of lost and found the angels cry
Ride
Ride until the darkness closes in
Until the ravaged soul begins to reflect the open skies
Ride

The chapel was burned
Razed to the ground
From the darkest of clouds
Small birds tumbled like rain
Time and again
You may go charging at windmills
In these days
Absurdities never change

Ride
Ride the very thought into the ground
In the church of lost and found the angels cry
Ride
Ride until the darkness closes in
Until the ravaged soul begins to reflect the open skies
Ride

In the thick of the woods the word is taboo
In the darkest of continents light can deceive you

Ride
Ride the very thought into the ground
In the church of lost and found the angels cry
Ride
Ride until the darkness closes in
Until the ravaged soul begins to reflect the open skies
Ride

Saddle up your thoughts and run to ground
In this world of lost and found the eagle flies
Ride

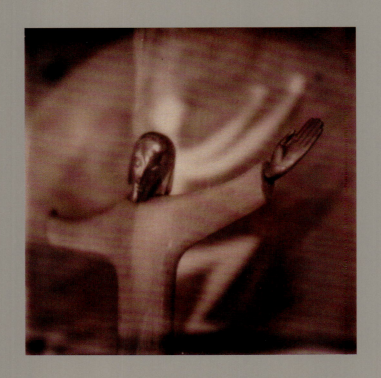

PLIGHT & PREMONITION

FLUX & MUTABILITY

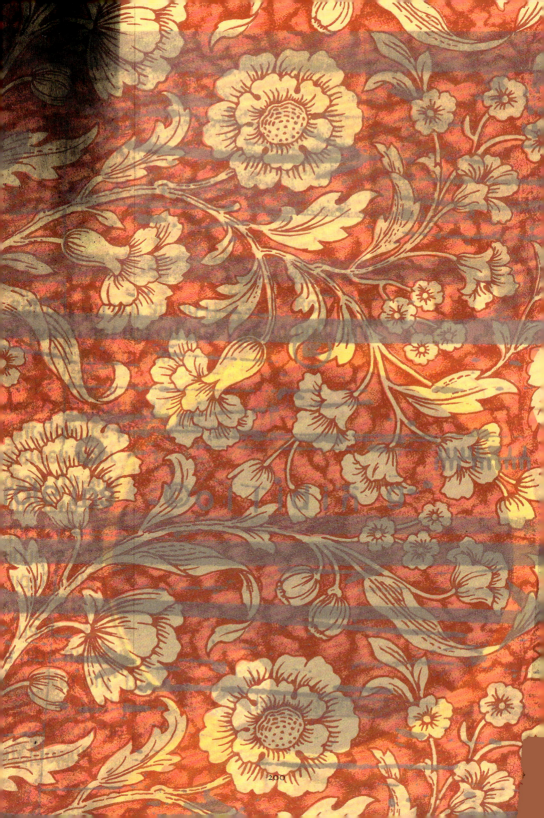

202

89/91 - RAIN TREE CROW

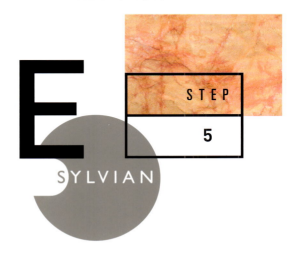

E

STEP

5

SYLVIAN

RAIN TREE CROW

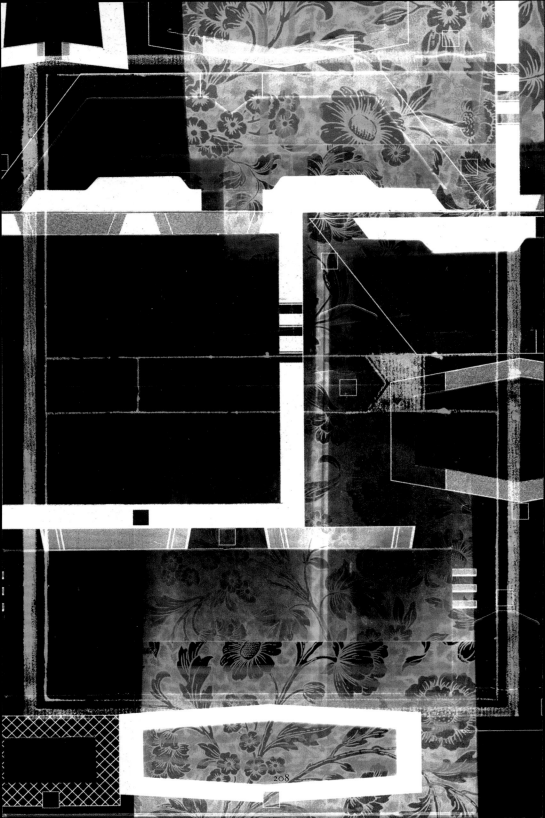

POP SONG

Behind the iron gates
The shifts were worked in silence
Each weekend beckoned like Ulysses' sirens
And as the words were few
We'd listen to the radio
It was loud and irritated me so

I'll tell you I love you
Like my favourite pop song

These promises won't keep
Though every road begins and ends with you
The fall still hurts, the bruise still blue
I'll paint you pictures of bright tomorrows
But the money goes and the time goes too

I'll tell you I love you
"Like the stars above you"
Like my favourite pop song

Wild, unwise, trivialised, untrue

We squander these gifts
Like another Sunday supplement
They're just so much cash in the hands of the government

I'll tell you I love you
Like my favourite pop song
Favourite pop song

A bitter conversation ending in

DIVORCE

BIG WHEELS IN SHANTY TOWN

EVERY COLOUR YOU ARE

I touched his hand
It burned like coal
I put paid to the devil
And I saw the mountain fall
Fall on

Feel like crying
The joke's gone too far
You can be anything you want
Every colour you are

A family man
His patience tried
Put a torch to his home
And warmed his hands by the fire
No greed, no desire

My road's uncrossed
White-lined and tarred
By believing in you
Every colour you are
Every colour you are

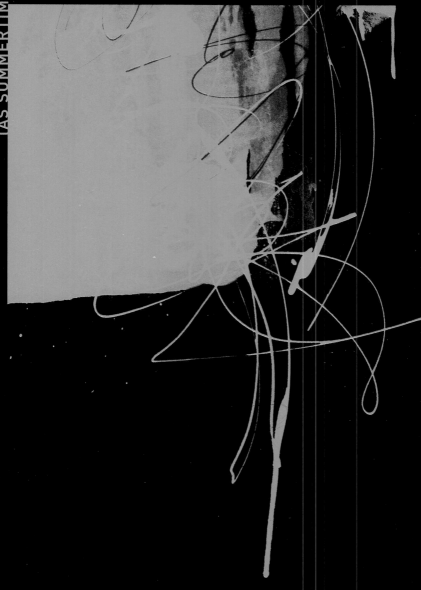

RAIN TREE CROW

I see the world with a heart that knows
In shadow play
Rain
Tree
Crow

I put no trust in milestones
Disparate hopes
Halfway homes
I share the world with one who knows
The light still shines in shadow play
Rain
Tree
Crow

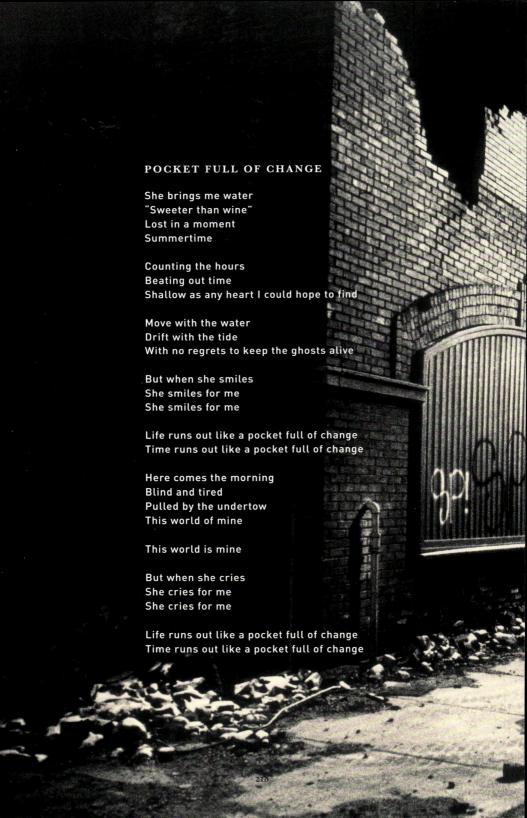

POCKET FULL OF CHANGE

She brings me water
"Sweeter than wine"
Lost in a moment
Summertime

Counting the hours
Beating out time
Shallow as any heart I could hope to find

Move with the water
Drift with the tide
With no regrets to keep the ghosts alive

But when she smiles
She smiles for me
She smiles for me

Life runs out like a pocket full of change
Time runs out like a pocket full of change

Here comes the morning
Blind and tired
Pulled by the undertow
This world of mine

This world is mine

But when she cries
She cries for me
She cries for me

Life runs out like a pocket full of change
Time runs out like a pocket full of change

NEW MOON AT RED DEER WALLOW

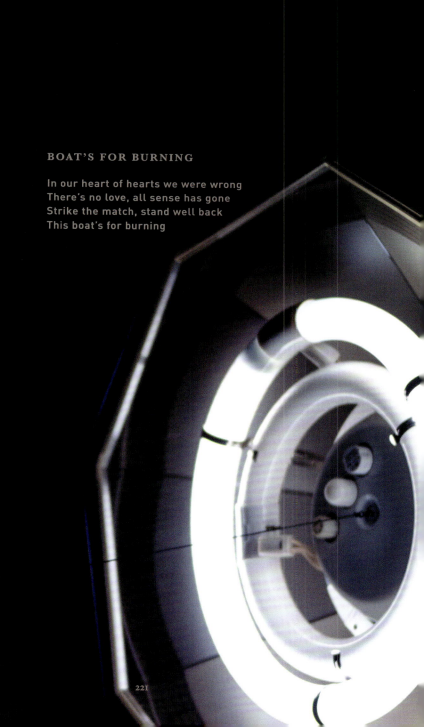

BOAT'S FOR BURNING

In our heart of hearts we were wrong
There's no love, all sense has gone
Strike the match, stand well back
This boat's for burning

BLACKWATER

I haul you in a sea of silence
On the borderline of truth
Hope and violence

I see no sun
I see no place I've loved
Depending on the signs to find the road

Blackwater
Take me with you
To the place that I have spoken
Come and lead me
Through the darkness
To the light that I long to see again

I walk with you
But sleep beside her
If summer came and went
It passed us over

I see her cry
I see the face I've loved
Depending on the blind to find the road

Blackwater
Take me with you
To the place that I have spoken
Come and lead me
Through the darkness
To the light that I long to see again

Blackwater
Take me with you
To the place that I have spoken
I am leaving in the morning
For the land that I long to see again

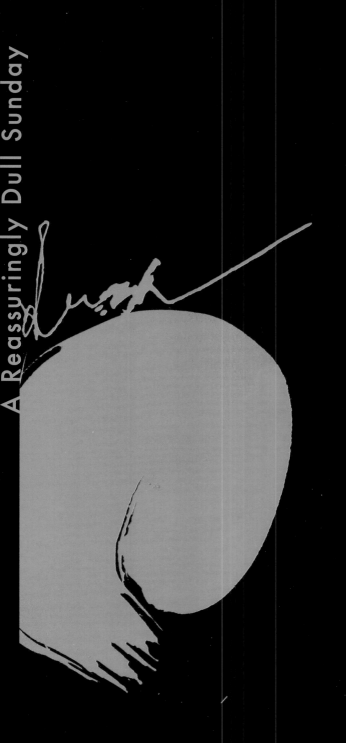

A Reassuring Dull Sunday

SCRATCHINGS ON THE BIBLE BELT

BLACKCROW HITS SHOE SHINE CITY

The beat of his wings
Under moon
Never tire
As Blackcrow descends
Stealing somebody else's fire

His suffering's no cause for pity
As Blackcrow hits Shoe Shine City

The gods burned his wings
Struck dumb for his crimes
Now Blackcrow descends on Shoe Shine

CRIES AND WHISPERS

A shattered dream on a bed of lies
Now my love dies in cries
Cries and whispers

My heart grew wings under desert skies
Now my love dies in cries
Cries and whispers

Cries and whispers

And my heart sings of many things
In cries and whispers

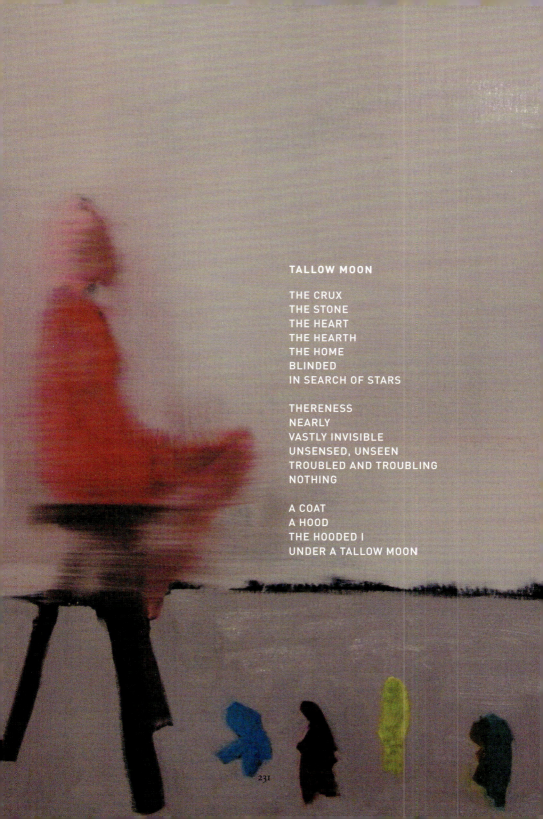

TALLOW MOON

THE CRUX
THE STONE
THE HEART
THE HEARTH
THE HOME
BLINDED
IN SEARCH OF STARS

THERENESS
NEARLY
VASTLY INVISIBLE
UNSENSED, UNSEEN
TROUBLED AND TROUBLING
NOTHING

A COAT
A HOOD
THE HOODED I
UNDER A TALLOW MOON

ENDGAME

I just sank into sleep
The conversation wasn't worth repeating
Faith would start the morning off
By judging love
She'd finally found me wanting

She said that I was born with one foot in the door
"Displays of affection but you don't know what it's for"

And Jesus said don't worry son
That's just the sound of God laughing

The room was quite a mess
The court said I had no defense against her
The bags were packed, the doors were closing
A three day truce of hostilities was over

I thought I'd notice when my tail was in the fire
She dressed the wounds with vitriol to keep the burns alive

And Jesus said if you listen good
You'll hear the sound of God laughing

Last chances in the car
The fine white lines are leading to the station
I'll start the journey off defining love
With a thousand explanations

Rows of telegraph poles
Where the railway meets the sea
Counting crucifixions on this road to Calvary

And the DJ said you've been listening to
The wonderful sound of God laughing

And Jesus said it's over once
You've heard the sound of God laughing

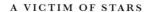

A VICTIM OF STARS

Words are blinded and the bows released
Lights tiny arrows pierce the moon
I turned the tallow in the hand of sleep
A victim of stars for want of a room

I raised the boat in a sea of sound
Astonished, absolutely spellbound.

A hungry heart in the house of bread
Stoned in anger at the garden fence
Hung from elms and shot with lead
A victim of stars without defense

I raised the boat in a sea of sound
Astonished, absolutely spellbound.

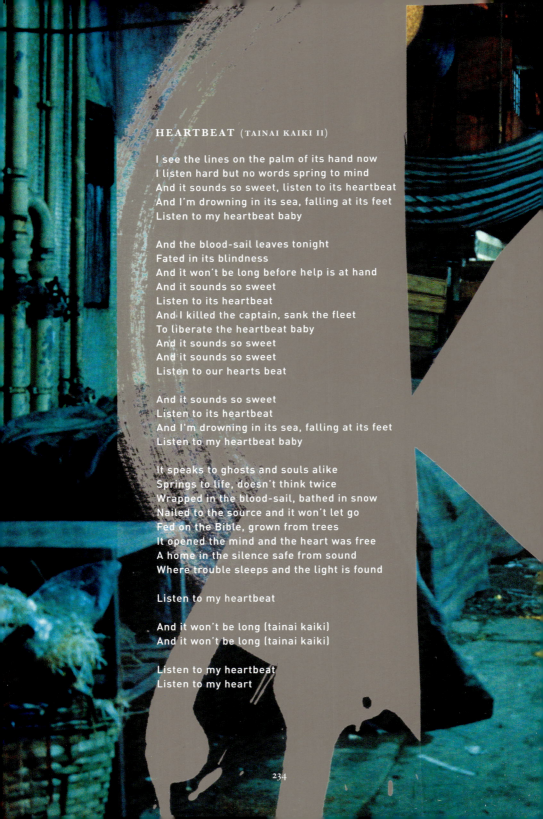

HEARTBEAT (TAINAI KAIKI II)

I see the lines on the palm of its hand now
I listen hard but no words spring to mind
And it sounds so sweet, listen to its heartbeat
And I'm drowning in its sea, falling at its feet
Listen to my heartbeat baby

And the blood-sail leaves tonight
Fated in its blindness
And it won't be long before help is at hand
And it sounds so sweet
Listen to its heartbeat
And I killed the captain, sank the fleet
To liberate the heartbeat baby
And it sounds so sweet
And it sounds so sweet
Listen to our hearts beat

And it sounds so sweet
Listen to its heartbeat
And I'm drowning in its sea, falling at its feet
Listen to my heartbeat baby

It speaks to ghosts and souls alike
Springs to life, doesn't think twice
Wrapped in the blood-sail, bathed in snow
Nailed to the source and it won't let go
Fed on the Bible, grown from trees
It opened the mind and the heart was free
A home in the silence safe from sound
Where trouble sleeps and the light is found

Listen to my heartbeat

And it won't be long (tainai kaiki)
And it won't be long (tainai kaiki)

Listen to my heartbeat
Listen to my heart

The Beekeeeper's Apprentice

Epiphany

92/93 - THE FIRST DAY

244

THE FIRST DAY

GOD'S MONKEY

One push
You fall in
Born in darkness
Born in darkness and
Built on shame
And hurting
Filled with silence
Filled with silence and
Stars
Stars
Stars

Find the ladder
Climb the ladder
To God's Monkey

No songs to sing
That I believe in
That I believe in and
Can't breathe the air
It's too thin
This far from heaven
This far from heaven and
Stars
Stars

Find the ladder
Climb the ladder
To God's Monkey

JEAN THE BIRDMAN

He gambles on the saddle
He's pulling at the mane
He thrashes at the horse's back
Ambition is a bloody game

Horse doesn't want to jump
The river looks too wide
Well he faces every hurdle
With a nervous state of mind

"Stay with me, breathe deeply
Take three paces back
Turn and make a full attack"

The gods are laughing
And they're tugging at the reins
But he's taken to his wings
And they hit the bank

Heaven may stone him
But Jean the birdman pulls it off

His finger's on the trigger
His eye is on the clock
He doesn't give the game away
And quickly fires the bullets off

Six hearts cut short
Still dreaming they're alive
Blown 'round in dusty circles
Like an absent state of mind

Who hunter, who victim?
God love America
He surely doesn't love him

Hitching out of nowhere
Lines of traffic knee deep
A chance to stave the morning off
And get some sleep

Heaven may stone him
But Jean the birdman pulls it off

He wears a crucifix
His mother left for him
It's wrapped in chains around his heart
Rusted and wafer thin

"Don't count on luck son"
All the angels sing
"Don't need to check the weathervane
We all know what tomorrow brings"

Life is a cattle farm
Coyotes with the mules
Life is a bullring
For taking risks and flouting rules

Who needs a safety net
The world is open wide
Just look out for the card sharks
And the danger signs

Heaven may stone him
But Jean the birdman pulls it off

FIREPOWER

He beats the door and breaks the lock
Raids the fridge and eats the lot
No room for silence, pause, or thought
To ease the hurt inside him

They placed the barrel at his head
Raging blind and rising
Cursed by saints and all the rest
He can't stand up for trying

Shot through with anger and desire
A mouth to feed, a room for hire
He drinks goodbyes, the bottle dry
Brutalised but smiling

Causing casualties by the hour
Outweighed by stars and firepower

Causing casualties by the hour
Waylaid by stars and firepower

He beats the door and breaks his watch
Afraid to sleep he won't let up
No room for silence, pause, or thought
To ease the hurt inside him

F.I.R.E.P.O.W.E.R.

BRIGHTNESS FALLS

Baby, baby I hate to go
Don't leave me alone in this sorrow

The body's heavy
The getting's slow
Lost in moments
Caught in moments
The night is starless
And stands below
And I need you by my side

Baby, baby I love you so
Don't leave me alone in this hollow

When brightness falls
Who'll come running?
When brightness falls
Who'll come running in?

Saved by silence
Saved by noise
Saved by lightning
Saved by joy
Building on emptiness
And all you broken hearted people

Baby, baby the hurt heals slow
And who can believe in tomorrow?

When brightness falls
Who'll come running?
When brightness falls
Who'll come running in?

The ticket's exploded
Only one way out
Live in lightness
Lost in lightness
There's nothing left to write about
And time's no longer the greatest injustice of all
On this new day

On this new day

TWENTIETH CENTURY DREAMING (A SHAMAN'S SONG)

Cold morning
Start of another day
Sleeping through the epilogue
Waking to the sound of rain
Driven to the crossroads where value's meaningless
What did you do to my faith in justice hope and happiness?

Social, economical, spiritual
I'm moving to the house of love

Take my fire
Take my food and water
Forget about those promises of social and social order
Lassoed by the cowboys
Tied down and it shows
Well I'm roping in those bad dreams
And selling off my working clothes

Social, economical, spiritual
I'm moving to the house of love

Gonna take a course of action to restore my sight
'Til the heart of motivation is filled with a golden light
They're hiding in the treetops
Tugging at my coat
But the power lines are falling down
And burning in the undergrowth

Social, economical, spiritual
I'm moving to the house of love

As the river runs
Tumbles and turns
You know you shouldn't stay
Or play the game again
But it could be different this time
You may win

Dreaming, dreaming lying down

I'm moving to the house of love

Here comes the dreaming

DARSHAN (THE ROAD TO GRACELAND)

Darshan

Two birds
One stone
One chance
Is thrown
Don't make mistakes

Two thieves
Strung up
One knife
One cut
Two doors
One shut

One light
One way
One road
To take
We stand and wait

From cool
To warm
From dusk
'Til dawn
From flux to form

Kneeling on the road to graceland

Kneeling on the road to graceland
To graceland

Darshan

257

DAMAGE

259

THE FIRST DAY

Bring out the stars
And fade to silence
Let the heart decide
And watch it grow

Ring out the bells
Trading in blindness
Fooled by kisses
Touched by wings

Shadowfall
And water fills the room
Bathed in moon-grey-blue

Baby came and spoke her name
With promises to call again
Swimming gold in a blackened sea
She troubles me, she troubles me

Counting the ways
To fall without landing
Stumbling into flight
Descent and slide

Compressing sound
From coal to diamond
Words are knotted tight
To chords that bind

Shadowfall
And water fills the room
Bathed in moon-grey-blue

Baby came and spoke her name
With promises to call again
Swimming gold in a shipwrecked sea
She troubles me, she troubles me

Received by the eye, believed by the word
Be seen to make haste when the soundings are heard
Don't discourage me

Whittling down the wood with the stone
If the boundary breaks I'm no longer alone
Don't discourage me

Bring out the stars
On the first day
The first day

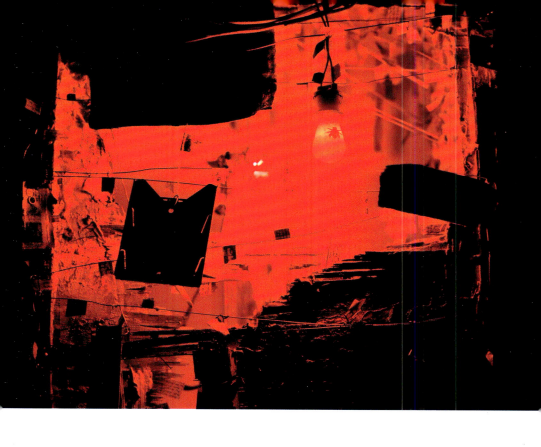

DAMAGE (BRINGING DOWN THE LIGHT)

I found the way
By the sound of your voice
So many things to say
But these are only words
Now I've only words
Once there was a choice

Did I give you much?
Well you gave me things
You gave me stars to hold
Songs to sing

I only want to be loved

And I hurt and I hurt
And the damage is done
You gave me songs to sing
Shadow and sun
Earthbound, starblind
Tied to someone

Why didn't I stay, why couldn't I?
So many lives to cross
Well I just had to leave
There goes everything
Everything

Can I meet you there?
God knows the place
And I'll touch your hand
Kiss your face

We only want to be loved
We only want to be loved
I only want to be loved

And I hurt and I hurt
And the damage is done
You gave me songs to sing
Shadow and sun
Earthbound, starblind
Tied to someone

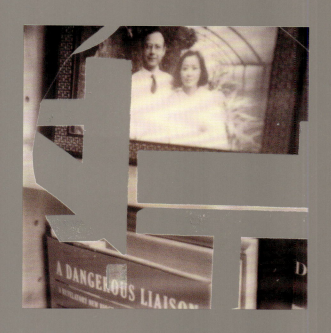

THE BLINDING LIGHT OF HEAVEN

I count the tables
She counts the trees
I tell her stories
She speaks of everything she sees
I'm in the shade
She's in the blinding light of heaven

The fire razed my paper boats
But now she stands before me
Opening the buttons of her coat
I find myself
Wrapped in the open arms of heaven

She's giving me everything she owns
Electricity

Now he has worked
These idle hands
I've turned my back
While she's done everything she can
I'd lie awake
Eaten by the poverty of anger

She's giving me directions home
I don't see a thing
Just this gentle glow of haloes

He told me of the grace I lacked
He clipped my wings
But now my strength is coming back
I lay my case
Before the open heart of heaven

She's telling me everything she knows
I don't hear a thing
Except this pylon-hum of haloes

She's telling me everything she knows
I don't hear a thing

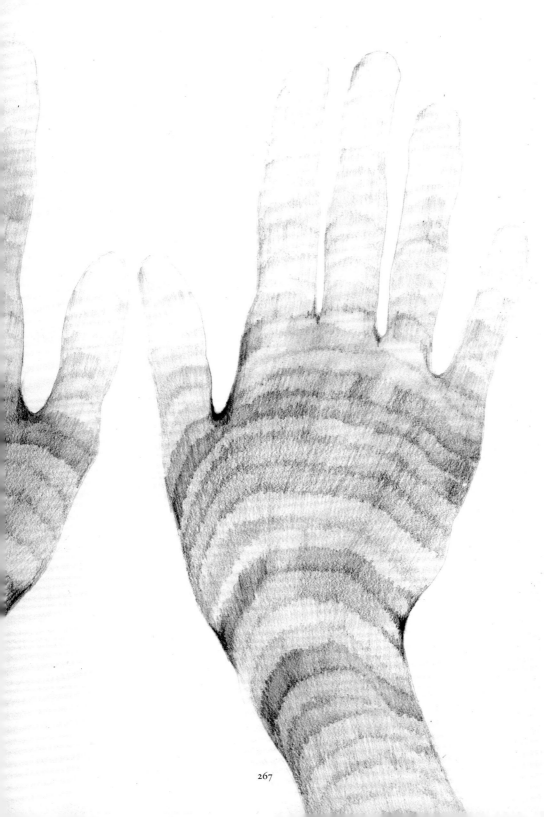

267

THE GOLDEN WAY

She said "Come to me and sit you down
You'll always return as I promised you would
When you're through playing games with the bad and the good
Immerse your heart in the remains of the day
On the golden way"

She's telling me stories of surrender and joy
Of warrior gods that the heavens deployed
And love that spills out from the words on the page
In this golden age

Shoot an arrow to Shiva
Through the blood of the sun
The prayers of a lifetime will not go unsung
On the golden way

The shadows emerge from night into day
And rally through lifetimes in anger and rage
But love embraces all
In the golden age

And the knife enters deep
But I'm longing to sing
The fool's ready to take the place of the king
It's the wildest of things

Destroyed and glistening
On silent wings

On the golden way

MAYA

Over there
The music's playing
Over there
The lights are shining
Over there
They need for nothing

Over there
Love's fires burning
Over there
The wheels stop turning
Over there
They need for nothing

Over there
The ships are sailing
Over there
The gods are crying
Over there
They need for nothing

COME MORNING

God is in the silences
Between the rhythm's rise and falling
The starring of the skies of blue
The promise of tomorrow's calling

Hey ho and away we go
Hey ho come morning

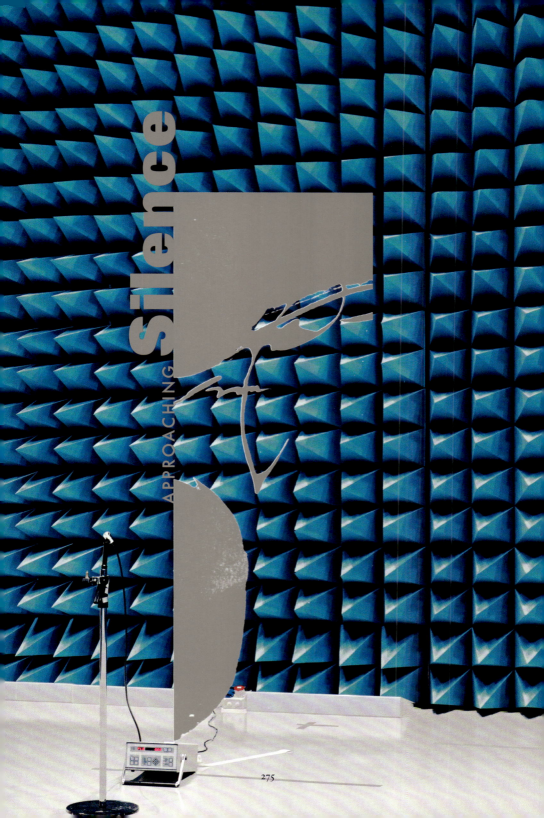

APPROACHING **Silence**

THE CHURCH BELLS STRIKE

AND RING DULLY INTO OUR COLLECTIVE SILENCE
A GENTLE CREAKING OF FLOORBOARDS
SPLINTERS FROM THE ROOM ABOVE
IN THE DISTANCE A DOG BARKS
A CAR CRUDELY KICKS UP ITS ENGINE AND PULLS AWAY
ALL ACTIVITY STRANGELY ANIMATED BY OUR STILLNESS

SILENCE ONCE MORE
THEN FOOTSTEPS

SHE'S BEGUN HER DESCENT
ACCOMPANIED BY THE SWEEP AND RUSTLE OF HER DRESS
IN ANTICIPATION WE TURN OUR HEADS
SO AS TO CATCH THE MUTED DRAMA OF HER ENTRANCE
AN EXPLOSION OF COLOUR AND LIGHT
A HUMMING, FAINT BUT DISTINCT
UNHEARD BUT ACKNOWLEDGED ALL THE SAME
AND NATURE BUZZES DRUNK ON THE BLOOD OF THE SUN
RADIATING LOVE PEACE AND COMPASSION
SHE IS AMONG US

277

SLOW FIRE

1. IN A GUNPOWDER NIGHT SKY
   SHOT THROUGH WITH HOLES
   SHE OFFERS UP HER SECRETS
   BLESSINGS FOR THE TAKING
   BONE SHATTERS SEAWARD
   SHIPS KEEL IN THE MIND-LIGHT
   THERE'S NO STOPPING HER

   SCATTERING DUST ON WIRES
   DOWN THE BLOODLINES

   SHE'S HERE AMONG US

2. I SAW YOU IN THE DROWNING
   FLAILING HELPLESSLY
   IN DEEP
   NO ONE AT HAND
   BUT SHE REACHED OUT AND PULLED YOU CLEAR
   OBLIVIOUS YOU LEAPT BACK INTO THE DARKNESS

3. IN THE UNBURDENED STILLNESS
   I COULD RECOGNISE THE BLISS
   THE SPIN OF IT ALL
   THE MATERNAL TOUCH OF MUNDANE MIRACLES
   GIDDY, LIGHTHEADED IN THE WHIRL AND THE RUSH
   I FLICKERED
   CANDLE-LIKE
   SUSPENDED IN THE NIGHT AIR
   SLOW FIRE DANCING
   THROUGH HER BOUNDLESS GRACE

4. ONWARDS
   SEEING IN THE BLINDNESS
   MAKING THE CURVE
   SPIRALING LADDER TO THE LIGHTHOUSE
   SHATTERED BY LOVE
   IN THE NEVER-MORE-THAN-NOW

SHADOWLAND

Shine upon my hour shadowland
Cold, cold winter hands
Shine upon my hour shadowland

Mountain weeping, mountain fall
Climbing up the charcoal trees
By God's grace she sings to me

Shine upon my hour
Shine upon my hour

And after dark who lays you down?
After dark who lays you down?

Starlight weeping, starlight fall
Shining up the amber leaves
By God's grace she sings to me

Shine upon my hour shadowland
Cold, cold winter hands

And after dark who lays you down?

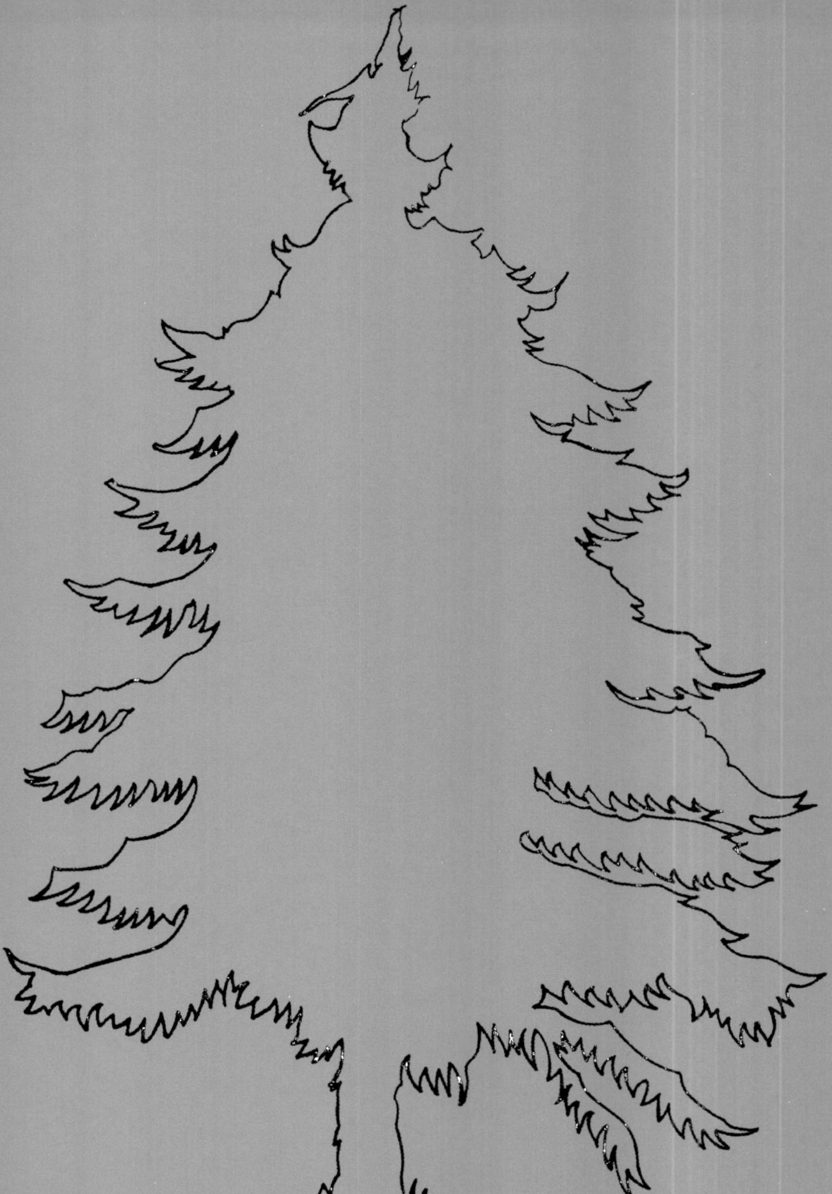

WHOSE TRIP IS THIS?

I'm holding onto nothing
But this love for life
Things really haven't turned out right
We're running at the wrong speed
Chasing the tails of time
All god's children holding back the light

Someday we're bound to wake up

And any fool could make it happen
Any fool could make it work
Sowing seeds back of compassion
Growing flowers in the earth

Who's swimming, waving, or drowning?
The silence grows more and more profound
Oh baby whose, whose trip is this?
I won't be blinded, the sun may be shining
But there's black clouds of smoke arising
Tell me whose, whose trip is it?

Oh tell me whose, whose trip is this?

Standing still amidst the madness
Gravity pulls you in
It's time to question everything you see
Who's to say we must be dreaming
Believing we all are free
'Cause dreams are what we're gonna need

Or else we'll never wake up

And any fool could make it happen
Any fool could make it work
Sowing seeds back of compassion
Growing flowers from the earth

Who's swimming, waving, or drowning?
The silence grows more and more profound
Oh baby whose, whose trip is this?
Moonlighting, families dogfighting
And it's patently all for nothing
Tell me whose, whose trip is it?

Oh tell me whose, whose trip is this?

It's not good enough to believe in change
When attitudes remain the same
Tell me whose, whose trip is this?

And I won't be rushed or dealt a hand
In somebody else's power plan
Oh baby whose, whose trip is this?

Won't somebody tell me because
I need to know now
Whose trip is it?

After all whose, whose trip is this?

Any fool can make it happen
Can make it work
All we need is some compassion
And the will to learn

Tell me, who, whose trip is this?
After all.

RECORDING ANGELS

I'm cornered on the edge of the board
Lost in the trick of the game
The edges dark
A black sun, cover blown
Burning in anger, burning in anger
And it's all the same
And I've seen these things
I've seen these things
And I'm writing them down
Between the spit and the spree
I'm writing it down

Recording angels
Recording angels
'Cause I believe in these things
I believe in these things
Recording angels

Among the stones
And the long black grass
They whisper sleep
But I can almost hear them
They say, "promise..."
And I fall
"Promise us you'll let them know"
And I said, "I swear to God I loved you
I didn't mean to let you go"
And I'm laughing
Between tears and a scream
But I write it down

Recording angels
Recording angels
'Cause I believe in these things
Yes, I believe in these things
Recording angels

Outlines on beaches
A thread is pulled and rain begins
Nets are hauled up from the sea
Counting fishes, countless fishes
I'm woven in the blue sky
Stitched up, feeling like a king
And I'm pulling feathers from their backs
Just to write it all down
'Cause I've seen these things

Recording angels

Preparing the blackboard
Chalked up from the notebook
Describing all of the places I didn't look
Stories of cities, kingdoms, and cars
And what I had found had always been there
From under the earth, the brilliance of stars

But I wrote it all down
From his head to his toes
Measured the wingspan
Stolen the clothes
'Cause I've seen these things
I believe in these things

We're holding the rope
That silenced the bells

Recording angels

LES FLEURS DU MAL

I'm sitting, waiting, repeating his name
When the embers and ashes of an open fire
Blaze into life
And Hanuman comes, takes my hand
His daughter, child, mother, wife
This is no rebirth
Beyond anything my mind can understand
There's all the love in the world here
All the love in the world
No defenses, well who's deceived?

I know the name of the woman
Who brought me into this world
And she'll be there when I leave

To be born out of darkness
Afloat on a river
With its belly of stones
Each signed and delivered
To rise from the conflict
Love the beloved
To pull ourselves up
And not run with the hunted

(Embrace the world then give it up)

Sitting in a long boat
Without a paddle or a sail
Children of the great indifference
Les fleurs du mal

A brilliant moon on the Ganges
Love songs and midnight fires
The water flows as white as milk
Limitless, with no desires

The day ended without any warning
They buried the sun down on the beach
Where it'll stay until morning

But I can still feel its heat
Through the soles of my feet

(Embrace the world then give it up)

Sitting in a long boat
Without a paddle or a sail
Children of the great indifference
Les fleurs du mal

BLUE SKINNED GODS

I'm inside, I'm out
And I don't know whose thoughts I'm thinking
I'd rationalise if I only had a clue
Yellow and red are the colours to which I swear allegiance
And I follow them back to you

And it's love, love, love
It's love
And it's love, love, love
It's love

Oh yeah, oh yeah
I'm living in the lap of the blue skinned gods
Oh yeah, oh yeah
I'm living in the lap of the blue skinned gods

She's filling the air with hibiscus and magnolia
The sandalwood trees lit like matches in the sun
She's singing her songs by the waters of the Ganges
She's saying "God is the only one"

And it's love, love, love
It's love
And it's love, love, love
It's love

Oh yeah, oh yeah
I'm living in the lap of the blue skinned gods
Oh yeah, oh yeah
I'm living in the lap of the blue skinned gods

She's whispering words that fall like pearls upon the water
I'm hearing of things you wouldn't believe were true
A thousand wings move to a voice and a tambura
And I follow them back to you

And it's love, love, love
It's love
And it's love, love, love
It's love

Oh yeah, oh yeah
I'm living in the lap of the blue skinned gods
Oh yeah, oh yeah
I'm living in the lap of the blue skinned gods

THE GREAT SWAN

How quietly the air is moving
The wind can barely sound the chimes
I recognise her now in all things
Reflections in and out of time

"If you want to walk with me
Live in truth" is what she says
And they want to walk with you
Well they would do wouldn't they?

The coming of the great swan
Born of love, the great swan
Born of love

There's an otherworldly silence
Playing out behind her smile
"You must face the world together
You must raise a different child"

"There's a place where I will be
You can look for me there
Now you are family, well are you happy?"

The coming of the great swan
Born of love, the great swan
The coming of the great swan
Born of love

294

ROOMS OF THE SIXTEEN SHIMMERS

There was light on their wings
As I slipped into the water
There was light on their wings

There was gold on their hands
As they pushed their weight upon me
There was gold on their hands

Multiplying in number all around me
The seven in addition to the nine

I won't wrestle, I won't fight
This is what the anchor taught me
I won't wrestle in the absence of light

Magnifying the thoughts that never leave me
The red is now reflected in the gold

I will hide among the ghosts
And the rooms of sixteen shimmers
I will listen while my secrets are told

There was love in their ways
And a face filled with indifference...

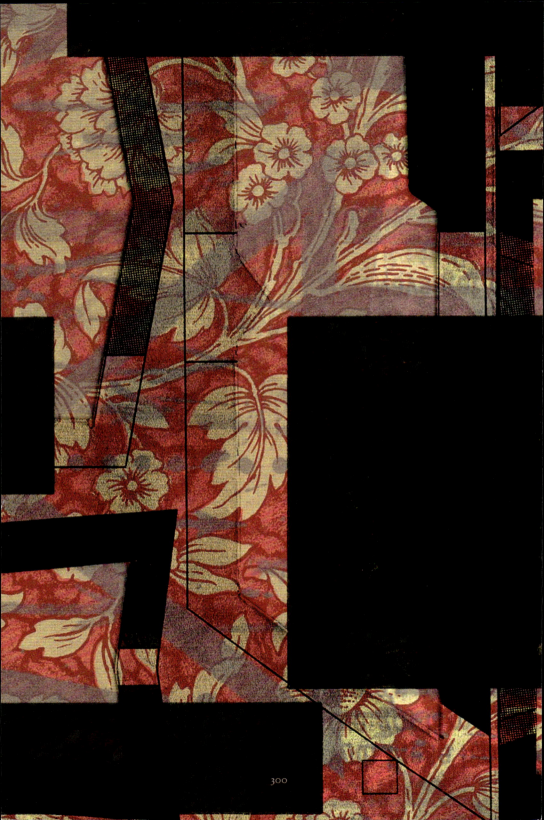

92/93 - DEAD BEES ON A CAKE

G

SYLVIAN

STEP

7

DEAD OR ALIVE DAVID SYLVIAN

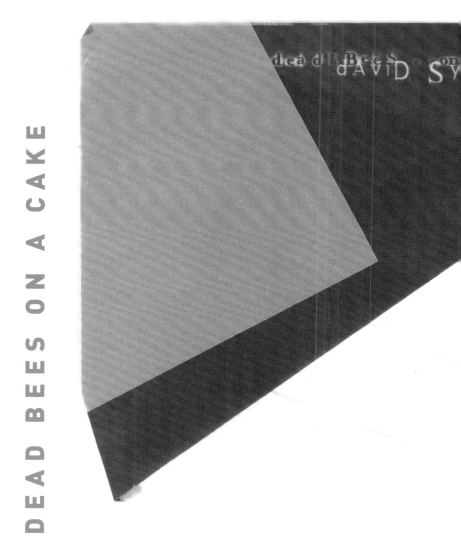

DEAD BEES ON A CAKE

I SURRENDER

I opened up the pathway of the heart
The flowers died embittered from the start

That night I crossed the bridge of sighs and I surrendered

I looked back and glimpsed the outline of a boy
His life of sorrows now collapsing into joy

And tonight the stars are all aligned and I surrender
My mother cries beneath a southern sky and I surrender

Recording angels and the poets of the night
Bring back the trophies of the battles that we fight

Searchlights fill the open skies and I surrender

Outrageous cries of love have called you back
Derailed the trains of thought, demolished wayward tracks

You tell me I've no need to wonder why I just surrender

I stand too close to see the sleight of hand
How she found this child inside the frightened man

Tonight I'm learning how to fly and I surrender

I've traveled all this way for your embrace
Enraptured by the recognition on your face

Hold me now while my old life dies tonight and I surrender
My mother cries beneath the open skies and I surrender

An ancient evening just before the fall
The light in your eyes the meaning of it all

Birds fly and fill the summer skies and I surrender

She throws the burning books into the sea
"Come find the meaning of the word inside of me"

It's alright the stars are all aligned and I surrender
My mother cries beneath the moonlit skies and I surrender

My body turns to ashes in her hands
The disappearing world of footprints in the sand

Tell me now this love will never die and I'll surrender
My mother cries beneath the open skies and I surrender

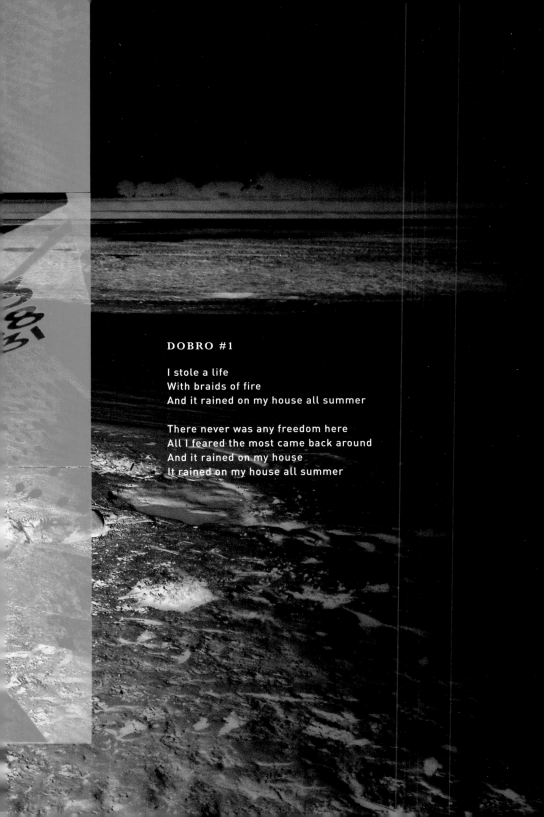

DOBRO #1

I stole a life
With braids of fire
And it rained on my house all summer

There never was any freedom here
All I feared the most came back around
And it rained on my house
It rained on my house all summer

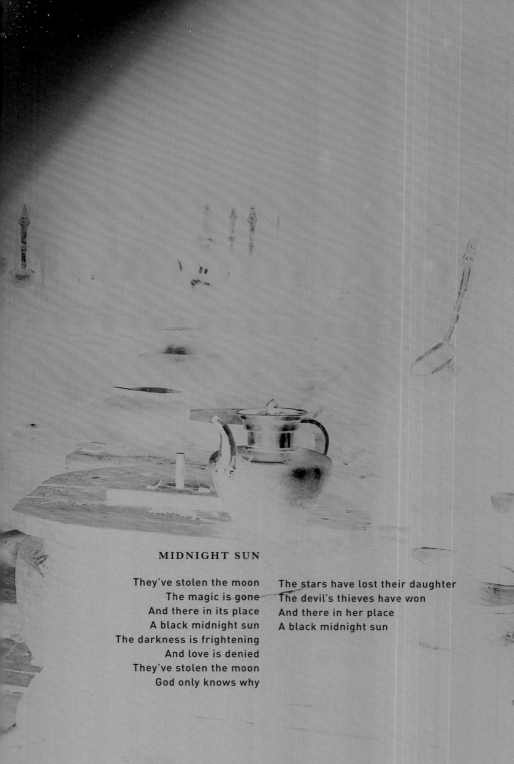

MIDNIGHT SUN

They've stolen the moon
The magic is gone
And there in its place
A black midnight sun
The darkness is frightening
And love is denied
They've stolen the moon
God only knows why

The stars have lost their daughter
The devil's thieves have won
And there in her place
A black midnight sun

314

DOG

315

THALHEIM

Couldn't leave you if I tried
Couldn't weather this alone
And through the darkness you still provide
The sweetest love I've ever known

Take the shadow from the road I walk upon
Be my sunshine, sunshine
And in the emptiness
You look and find someone
The damage is undone
And love has made you strong
Heaven gave me mine

Thalheim

The saddest words have come undone
Changing the very air I breathe
And miracles have just begun
In which only you and I believe

Take the shadow from the road I walk upon
Be my sunshine, sunshine
And in the weightlessness
You look and find someone
The damage is undone
And love has made you strong
Heaven gave me mine

Thalheim

When I'm all at sea
You never let me down
I'll just keep coming back to you
'Til I walk on solid ground

From the foothills to the mountains
On the waters of the Rhine
Face to face in Shahbagh gardens
In communion, out of time

Thalheim

From the lilies of the valley
To the grapes upon the vine
The well of speculation
Is it his or hers or mine?

Thalheim

In the everything and nothing
In disharmony and rhyme
In the sound of shot and echo
Who's the victim, what's the crime?
What's the crime?

Be my, oh be my sunshine

In the keening cries of evening
Unforgotten, underlined
We slipped into the water
Out of focus, out of time.

316

GODMAN

Welcome to Sun State
The language of light
The energy's impulse
The loud, dark, iron
The purpose of history
The Eurasian steppes
From threshold to threshold
Astonishment

You've misunderstood the place where you stand
Godman

You've misunderstood the place where you stand
Godman

From different maps
Dead bees on a cake
You're sweeping the forest
Man, it's getting late
The milkweed is growing
Through cotton grass
You borrowed the car
But you didn't ask

You've misunderstood the place where you stand
Godman

When everything's dark
You're wrapped up
Born into brightness

You've misunderstood the place where you stand
You've misunderstood the place where you stand

ALPHABET ANGEL

It's later than I thought it was
The shadows long and lost
Circle through the room
Swear as I met your mother there
In New Orleans
The sun was slipping into blue

The longest day is over
The longest day

My alphabet angel's come out to play

KRISHNA BLUE

She's here in the snowfall
At dead of night
The mood is of courtship
The final fight
She's all that I need
All that I am
The voice of compassion inside the man

If you open the gates
The madness begins
I'll follow you down
I'll follow you back in
She's here in the lifelines
In every curve
Suspended in silence
Between each word

It's all in the way that she moves
The grace and the light that will see me through
It's coming true
She's prising the rope from my hands
The fear and the hopes that I held onto
It's coming true
Colour the river I swim back to you
Krishna blue

Waist deep in water
She starts to sing
The voice is familiar
And draws me in
She's lighting the fires
I dowsed by hand
Erasing the figure drawn in sand

You open the gates
The madness begins
I follow you down
I follow you back in
And here in the darkness
The boundary gone
The flame is alive
And burning strong

It's all in the way that she moves
The grace and the light that will see me through
It's coming true
Colour the river I swim back to you
Krishna blue

In the softest belly
And the warmest heart
In your open hands
I lay my head
In the never-ending
I fall apart
In the silent forest
And the brilliant red
And through the stream of words
There comes a sound
And I listen
Child-like
To her voice
Spellbound

It's all in the way that she moves
The grace and the light that will see me through
It's coming true
She's prising the rope from my hands
The fear and the hopes that I held onto
It's coming true
Colour the river I swim back to you
Krishna blue

THE SHINING OF THINGS

Take my word for it this never should've happened
What in the world do you think got into me?
We fire at will and as we watch the pieces shatter
We find we're closer than we've ever been

She calls my name and I come running
I have lost the voice I listened to
And in the blindness as my world stops turning
There's a sadness like I never knew

But I still see the shining of things

As the morning breaks it hardly seems to matter
I hear a shallowness in everything I say
We've played the night out in all too familiar fashion
To wear the heartache through another day

She calls my name and I come running
I have lost the voice I listened to
And there's a stillness now the rain's stopped falling
And there's a sadness like I never knew

But I see the shining of things

CAFÉ EUROPA

They fired off the first shot
So we're on our feet and running
We're re-writing all the text books
In the process of becoming
We've so much to live for
If we stop putting up a fight
There's a place for every story
And this one starts with us tonight

Let me take you down
To Café Europa
There's so much to be found
So much to discover
Let me take you down
To Café Europa
There's so much to be found

I won't let you down

We're traveling by moonlight
From London to the Highlands
We lose ourselves in inner cities
In the hope of re-defining
The space that surrounds us
Or the emptiness within
It's all in the papers
The boy's in love again

Always arriving
Headlights lit up from coast to coast
Empty days full to bursting
With the names of the people and places
We miss the most

I'm taking the last train
Flying my last flight
I'm calling on the angels
They're letting in the sunlight

Let me take you down
To Café Europa
There's so much to be found
So much to discover
Let me take you down
To Café Europa
There's so much to be found

I won't let you down

It's the heart that has been broken
Finds the truth in what is spoken

POLLEN PATH

Welcome me father
On the north shores of Lapland
Welcome me father
Who knows no name
Welcome me mother
The earth here is yawning
My body is shaking
For want of a flame

Down here
Got to laugh
The kick back is lightening
Drowning
Got to laugh
This whole mess is frightening

I follow the pollen path
The pollen path

Welcome me father
The lava is rising
Welcome me mother
And give me your name

We've drunk from this wellspring
Too long, too long
Dividing the hours
To measure the time

We've lived with this heartache
Too long, too long
Numbering what's yours, what's mine

We've harboured this sadness
So long
Nursing a voice
To sing us our songs

Raising a voice
To sing our songs

All Of My Mother's Names

WANDERLUST

Help me
I feel like I'm weightless
Floating right out of your hands

And there's only so much I aspire to
Taking one day at a time
And deliverance has many faces
But grace is an acquaintance of mine
Tell me, how could it have happened?
You know that we're not the marrying kind
Travel light, don't think twice
We're leaving the shadows behind

It's given us this wonderful wanderlust
It's given us this wonderful wanderlust
It's given us this wonderful wanderlust
I don't doubt it, I feel it

Wanderlust
Wanderlust

Help me
This waterboy's wasted
Falling right out of your sky

And there's nothing I could do without here
Loving the state that I'm in
Between no longer and not yet
On the threshold of some brighter thing
The match was struck and I was fire
The embers of a drowning man
Tell me why won't I listen
Or acknowledge that I don't understand?
Losing light, the selfish kind
And we're out on the road again

It's given us this wonderful wanderlust
It's given us this wonderful wanderlust
It's given us this wonderful wanderlust
I don't doubt it, I feel it

Turn the headlights on full
I want to take in it all
And let it wash over me

The bridge looked so high
From the banks that we climbed
But we climbed them so that we could be free

Give me no dreams of what the future brings
I need to know when I have gone too far

Repeated lightning strikes
Up and down the spine
They search us out wherever we are

In a world full of lies
That tug at the truth
I'm taking no sides
Now I recognise you

It's given us this wonderful wanderlust
I don't doubt it, no.

333

DARKEST DREAMING

Stay tonight
We'll watch the full moon rising
Hold on tight
The sky is breaking

I don't ever want to be alone
With all my darkest dreaming
Hold me close
The sky is breaking

I don't ever want to be alone
With all my darkest dreaming
Hold me close
The sky is breaking

The Song Which Gives the Key to Perfection

COVER ME WITH FLOWERS

Hold your head up sonny boy
Let the earth dry on it
It won't hurt you
It won't hurt you

Tell me something sonny boy
Baptised and plunged
Is it worth it?
It must be worth it

Hold your head up sonny boy
It won't hurt you
It won't hurt

Let's renew the promise
Break our wings upon it
If in peace there's power
Cover me with flowers

Tie your shoelace little girl
Time is waiting on it
And when it's over
And when it's over...?

I can offer nothing
This nothing's everlasting
I could be Shiva lying
Beneath ferocious darkness
My heart's devoured
Cover me with flowers

Let me see the face of all enduring grace
Let me take a crack at all that matters
And in the weightless hours
Cover me with flowers

Cover me with flowers

ALBUQUERQUE (DOBRO #6)

He arrives by night
Open up the door and let him in
She's the sole proprietor
Exchanging two for one
She's the sole proprietor
There is no other

Who would've thought she's in Albuquerque
When mother calls he must come
Out of hiding, remembers nothing

He takes the bus
Shades of mid-life crisis
Eyes of petrochemical blue

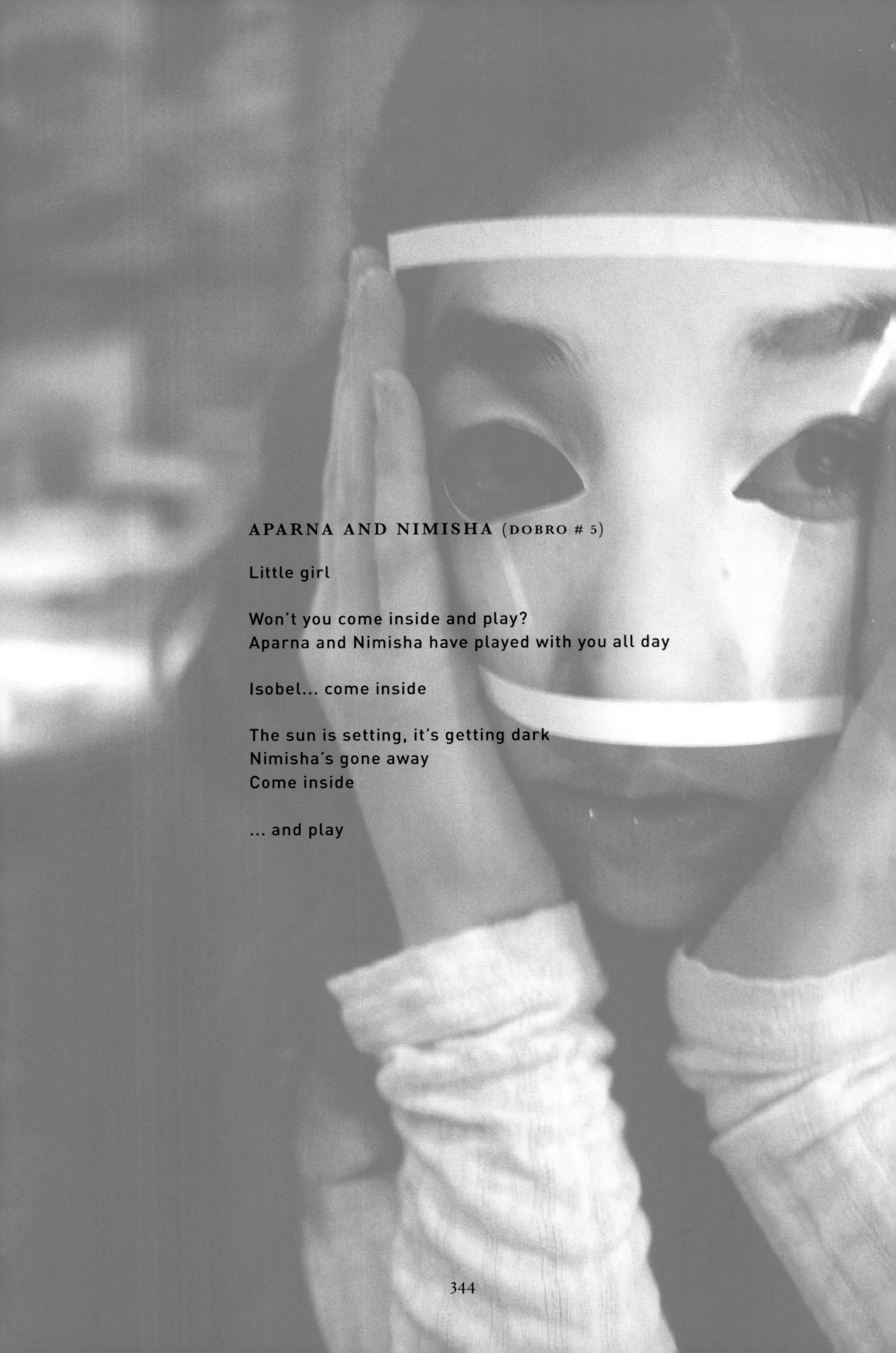

APARNA AND NIMISHA (DOBRO # 5)

Little girl

Won't you come inside and play?
Aparna and Nimisha have played with you all day

Isobel... come inside

The sun is setting, it's getting dark
Nimisha's gone away
Come inside

... and play

I DO NOTHING

He recognised the way she moved
Her hand on the water
The fire burning in the hull
The ferryman's daughter

Hallelujah
Is that what she's saying?
Hallelujah
The gods are playing

He didn't feel the lightning strike
How long was he waiting?
An echo rising deep from the heart
The sound of its breaking

Not even one more night
Spent here without her
Not even one more night
Sold down the river

The morning raised a million suns
How long was he sleeping?
All his stories shattered at once
Beginnings and endings

Not even one more night
Spent here without her
Not even one more night
Lost in the breakers

I do nothing and nothing is left undone
I do nothing and nothing is left undone

"Remove the blindfold and you'll see the danger's gone
The flower's growing from the stone
Like they told you it would"

Not even one more night
Spent without you

Hallelujah
Is that what she's saying?
Hallelujah
The gods are playing

I do nothing and nothing is left undone

WHEN THE LITTLE ONE CAME
A HOLE WAS BLOWN OPEN
A PARTIAL SURRENDERING IN THE MIDST OF KNOWING
AND FOR AN INSTANCE THE CONSTANT HEART SHED ITS OWN TEARS
WAVE UPON WAVE CARRIED ME OVER
BEYOND THE PERIPHERIES OF HOPE AND FEAR
DEADENING THE VOICE OF RELENTLESS BIOGRAPHY
I STOOD AT THE CENTER AND DANCED AT THE EXTREMITIES
MAPPING THE CITY AS SUBTLE AS SILENCE
THEN ON, OUTWARDS, INTO THE DARKNESS

WHEN THE CRAZY ONE CAME
SHE PLACED HER FINGER ON MY FOREHEAD
AND PUSHED ON THROUGH
I WOKE UP, FACE ON FIRE
SPITTING OUT DIAMONDS
THOROUGHLY LOST TO LOGIC
CRAVING HER MADNESS

347

Camphor

THE GOLD AND CRIMSON TULIP

BROUGHT FORTH A GODDESS
SHE STOOD BEFORE ME, BEES BUZZING
BENEATH AN EVENING SKY
ALL TIME
HERE
AS THE ROSE REACHES THE HAND
A THOUSAND VOICES SING THE SILENCE
THE WORK OF PLANETS UNFOLDING
A GLIMPSE OF THE MAP OF DESTINY IS MINE
MY FEET BURN THEIR IMPRINT IN STONE
NOW IT IS DONE

SHE BLOWS A HOLE THROUGH SOLID AIR
WHISPERS MY TRUE NAME
A CALLING CARD FROM THE HEARTS OF PRAYER

SHE IS ALL MOUNTAINS
HER BLACK EYES FATHOMLESS
ABSOLUTE STILLNESS
SILVER SHOOTING STARS GARLAND HER HAIR
HOW COULD THIS HOUSE CONTAIN ALL SHE IS?
SHE STANDS NEITHER WITHIN NOR WITHOUT
SOOTHING FIRE
SHE'S IN THE BELLY, THE HEAD, THE HEARTH
HER LAUGHTER PERVADES EVERYTHING
CLEANSING FIRE
LEAVE NOT ONE STONE UNTURNED

QUEEN BEE
SHE POLLINATES THE HEARTS OF ALL WHO COME
SHE IS ALL SUNS

I WILL LEARN TO WALK
I WILL LEARN TO BREATHE AS I ONCE DID
I WILL LEARN TO SING
AND SINGING I WILL WORSHIP YOU

SNAKES AND LADDERS

HOW INTIMATELY YOU MUST KNOW THE FLAMES
HOW THOROUGH THE LIGHT OF PURIFICATION
SNAKES AND LADDERS
SLOW FIRE OF ILLUMINATION
WHEN WERE YOU DONE WITH IT
SKIN KALI-DARK
HAIR CHARCOAL AND ASH?

WHO WAS THERE TO BATHE YOU
MASSAGE YOUR FEET
WRAP YOU IN SAFFRON AND KUM KUM
FEED YOU, BIND YOU TO US WITH DEVOTION
GARLAND YOU WITH MARIGOLDS?

WHERE ARE THE GARDENS IN WHICH YOU SLEPT
WHILST ALL CREATION WATCHED OVER YOU
AND JAPA FLOWED EFFORTLESSLY?

MOON KISSED MOUNTAIN
THE MOON, THE KISS, AND THE MOUNTAIN
SHE WHO WALKS WITHOUT MOVING
ALL OCEANS RETURN TO YOU
HOW COULD THEY NOT?
THE EARTH KNOWS THE TOUCH OF YOUR FEET
DAKSHINESWAR SPEAKS YOUR NAME

SUGARFUEL

There are many rooms
And many faces
When you're on the run
You run out of places
I'm on your side
I am your sugarfuel
I'll find where it hurts
I'll be the wound in you

I'm on your side

And when the drugs take hold
I will touch you
I will touch you
And when the words fall short
I will kiss you
I will kiss...

I'm on your side
So let me punish you
I'm on your side
I'll be your sugarfuel
When all your thoughts are dark
And all your dreams are blue
I'm with you

You're on your stomach
You can't speak
You're suffocating in this heat
Well if we suffer is that wrong
What doesn't kill us makes us strong

Were you pushed or did you slip
I'm tasting blood upon your lips
The door is locked, the floor is greased
And if your screams should break the peace
I'm on your side

So let me finish you

I'm on your side
So let me punish you
I'm on your side
I'll be your sugarfuel
When all your thoughts turn dark
And all your dreams

I'm with you, sugar
When all your thoughts are dark
And all your dreams are blue
I'm with you

THE DARK GLASS OF A GIRL

She'll get along somehow
Until night follows day
And carries her off with a word
She'll get along
She'll lower her voice to be heard

Who said that the ideal of innocence
Is one that is easily crushed?

And then it's done

The birds and chrysanthemums
That followed her here
Fall loose with a shake
Like the braids from her hair

And then it's done

So breathe just breathe
Place your mistrust with me 'til morning comes
And sleep just sleep
In the absence of dreams the nightmares come
And then it's done

The heart shape of the world
Through the dark glass of a girl
All the troubled oceans in the shell
Of the dark glass of a girl

She'll get along somehow
In the language of one
Whose birthplace went up in flames
She'll get along
The alphabet starts with her name

Her fingernails tear at the orange skin
She's dropping the fruit to the floor
And then it's done

The world at her letterbox
Is crying out loud
She fires both her guns straight into the crowd
And then it's done

So breathe just breathe
Place your mistrust with me til' morning comes
And sleep just sleep
In the absence of dreams the nightmares come
And then it's done

The heart shape of the world
Through the dark glass of a g rl
See the bruises where she fell
The dark heart of a girl
All the troubled oceans in the shell
Of the dark glass of a girl

GONE FROM THE LANDSCAPE

SNOW HAS SHOWN UP HERE
ON THE INTERIOR
BLANKETING EVERYTHING
I TRACE MY OWN PRINTS
OVER AND OVER
NUMB
DENIAL GIVING WAY TO RESIGNATION
MY HEART MUST BE WOUNDED
IT LENDS THE SNOW THE DEEPENING BLUSH OF ITS BLOOD

358

WORLD CITIZEN

There goes one baby's life
It's such a small amount
She's un-American
I guess it doesn't count

Six thousand children's lives
Were simply thrown away
Lost without medicine
Inside of thirty days

In the New York harbour
Where the stock's withheld
It was the price we paid for a safer world

World is suffering
World is suffering
World is suffering
World citizen

In Madhya Pradesh
Where they're building dams
They're displacing native peoples
From their homes and land

So they hunger strike
'Cause they believe they count
To lose a single life
Is such a small amount

In the name of progress and democracy
The concept's represented in name only

His world is suffering
Her world is suffering
Their world is suffering
World citizen

And the buildings fall
In a cloud of dust
And we ask ourselves
How could they hate us?
Well when we live in ignorance and luxury
While our superpowers practice
Puppet mastery

We raise the men
Who run the fascist states
And we sell them arms
So they maintain their place

We turn our backs
On the things they done
Their human rights record and the guns they run

His world is suffering
Her world is suffering
Their world is suffering
World citizen

My world is suffering
Your world is suffering
Our world is suffering
World citizen

Who'll do away with flags
Who'll do us proud
Remove the money from their pockets
Scream dissent out loud?

'Cause God ain't on our side
The shoe won't fit
And though they think the war is won
That's not the last of it

Disenfranchised people
Need their voices heard
And if no one stops to listen
Lose their faith in words

And violence rises
When all hope is lost
Who'll embrace the human spirit and absorb the cost?

(Not one life is taken in my name
In my name)

His world is suffering
Her world is suffering
Their world is suffering
World citizen

My world is suffering
Your world is suffering
Our world is suffering
World citizen

Not one life is taken in our name
In our name

WORLD CITIZEN (I WON'T BE DISAPPOINTED)

What happened here?
The butterfly has lost its wings
The air's too thick to breathe
And there's something in the drinking water

The sun comes up
The sun comes up and you're alone
Your sense of purpose come undone
The traffic tails back to the maze on 101

And the news from the sky
Is looking better for today
In every single way
But not for you

World citizen

World citizen

And it's not safe
All the yellow birds are sleeping
'Cause the air's not fit for breathing
It's not safe

Why can't we be
Without beginning, without end?
Why can't we be...

World citizen

World citizen

And if I stop and talk with you awhile
I'm overwhelmed by the scale of everything you fee
The lonely inner-state emergency

I want to feel
Until my heart can take no more
And there's nothing in this world I wouldn't give

I want to break
The indifference of the days
I want a conscience that will keep me wide awake

I won't be disappointed
I won't be disappointed
I won't be

I saw a face
It was a face I didn't know
Her sadness told me everything about my own

Can't let it be
When least expected there she is
Gone the time and space that separates us

And I'm not safe
I think I need a second skin
No, I'm not safe

World citizen

World citizen

I want to travel by night
Across the steppes and overseas
I want to understand the cost
Of everything that's lost
I want to pronounce all their names correctly

World citizen

World citizen

I won't be disappointed
I won't be

She doesn't laugh
We've gone from comedy to commerce
And she doesn't feel the ground she walks upon

I turn away
And I'm not sleeping well at night
And while I know this isn't right
What can you do?

03/05 - BLEMISH

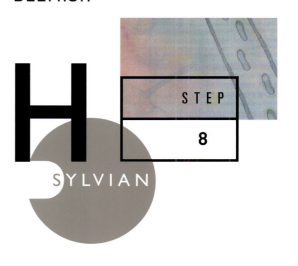

H

SYLVIAN

STEP

8

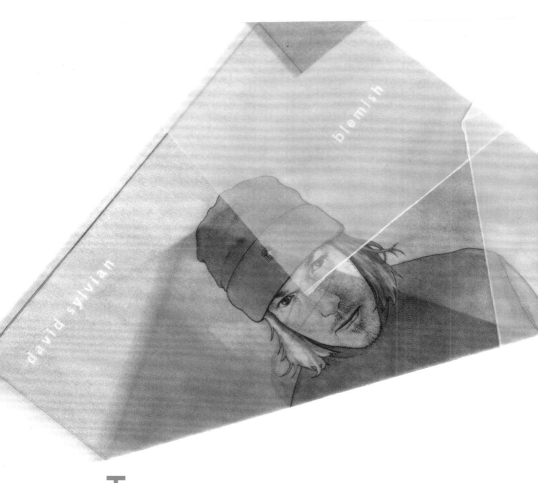

david sylvian

blemish

BLEMISH

373

BLEMISH

I fall outside of her
She doesn't notice
I fall outside of her
She doesn't notice at all

And mine is an empty bed
I think she's forgotten
And mine is an empty bed
She's forgotten I know

Put the brakes on
Put the brakes on
'Cause I'm fading fast
Can't find the link
Between me and her

He who was first's coming in last

I fall outside of her

And the trouble is there's no telling
Just who's right or who's wrong

Don't tell me that love is all there is
I know don't I?

Don't crowd me pappy
Got too much to think about
The game's not lost if I say it's not
And it's not
Give me one more chance to do things right
Don't crowd me pappy
Got too much to think about

There's no talking to her
Talking to her
I'll keep my thoughts to myself
Unless I'm asked

Like blemishes upon the skin
Truth sets in

Life's for the taking so they say
Take it away

I fall outside of her
She doesn't notice
She doesn't notice at all
And mine is an empty bed
I think she's forgotten

All is bloated and far from truth
Let's secure that reputation
Place the dummy upon the roof
Stitch him a tongue
Give him proof

Don't tell him love is all there is
I know, I know
Just pull the wool down over his eyes
One more time

Her heart's a foreign place
I visited for a while
And although I tried to please her
She came at night and stole my visa

Come away now, run away now little man
You'll not make sense of it
Try as you might to understand

Like blemishes upon the skin
Truth sets in

THE GOOD SON

You know he'll take you
But not too far
Always first in line
Second to none
The good son

The good son

He loves a good tune so whistle one he knows
He looks to you to see things right

So take this ring and pass it on
There's always stories riddled with lies
You know the questions are best put aside
Listen to him
Listen closely now here he comes

It's a shameful way to behave
It'll hurt if he gets his own way

You know he'll take you
But not too far
Always first in line
Second to none
Listen closely now
Listen closely now
Here he comes
The good son

He tells himself it's too far to come
To redefine his aspirations to be
The good son
The good son
The good son

"Don't try to make sense of it," she said
"It's all that you can do to balance up the books for him and you."

And though he's nothing in particular
He's game for a fight
He muscles his way in and stays for life

And all the world has come undone
And every family should have one
A good son

THE ONLY DAUGHTER

She was, she was
A friend of mine
Do us a favour, your one and only warning
Please be gone by morning

She was, she was
A friend of mine

Inconsistencies
Words on paper
The track still warm
I came to hate her

Smitten no longer
Me, the only daughter
Render the vow
It's my home now

This, your one and only warning
Please be gone by morning

And if the ending is clean
The quirk, the fuss, the Vaseline
She won't even see it coming
Roll them, roll them over, roll them over
Me, the only daughter

She was, she was
A friend of mine

Smitten no longer
Me, the only daughter
Render the vow
It's my home now

The penny's dropped
The room's in order
I masked the spot
Me, the only daughter

Do us a favour, your one and only warning
Please be gone by morning

THE HEART KNOWS BETTER

I don't know how long
She's been here with me
But it's been a long time coming

Make it last forever
Make it last forever
Yes, it's been a long time coming

There's a name for this one
There's a name for that
Call me by my true name
I'll call you back
But I've no intention of seeking you out

And the mind's divisive
But the heart knows better-ha
Better-ha

And every night is wedding night in my bed
My eyes are closed but I can see
The sky stretched overhead
The mattress on the floor
A sea of faces at my door
And every night is wedding night and I'm set

And the mind's divisive
But the heart knows better-ha
Better-ha

When she whispered in my ear
What did she say?
She put her hand hard on my chest
What did she say?
Oh, but nothing really matters in the end
And if everything still matters what then?

And the air is humid and my face is wet
And the driver's much too drunk to see
But she's sitting in my place
Devastating beauty in my place
And I'm absent from the place I ought to be

And the mind's divisive
But the heart knows better-ha
Ha-ha-ha

SHE IS NOT

There she is among her children
Full of paintings
Going round and round the houses
Full of paintings, full of pictures
There she is not

LATE NIGHT SHOPPING

Ask me I might go
Why not take me with you?
Ask me I might go
Late night shopping

We can take the car
No one will be watching
We can lose ourselves
Late night shopping

Tell me what we need
Write a list or something
We don't need to need a thing
Late night shopping

HOW LITTLE WE NEED TO BE HAPPY

She fell
No jewels for the hurt where she fell
Where is the mother?

Throw back the sheets
Shake off the sleep and complete me
As I complete you
There's a universe of disappointment to be lost

How little we need to be happy
How little we need to be really happy

And you my girl, did I forget to sing?
You, brimming with life and with joy
And curiosity

And the lights won't go out
The stars refuse to dim
And everything goes on but not as before

"They removed his voice
And the silence overwhelmed him"
How little it takes

Some of us are undecided
We might come to you
To find a new way out of this one
She should pull us through

What have they done to you?
Come here let me hold you
Cry all your tears
The sorrows that threaten to overwhelm you

Let's rise up again

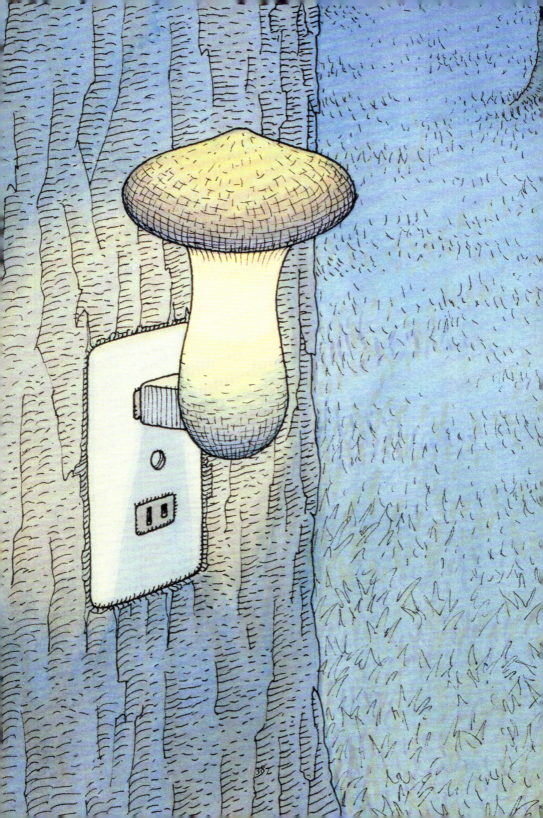

A FIRE IN THE FOREST

There is always sunshine
Above the grey sky
I will try to find it
Yes, I will try

My mind has been wandering
I hardly noticed
It's running on its own steam
I let it go
Oh here comes my childhood
A penny for your secrets
It's standing in the window
Not out here where it belongs

There's a fire in the forest
It's taking down some trees
When things are overwhelming
I let them be
I would like to see you
It's loverly to see you
Come and take me somewhere
Come take me out

There is always sunshine
Far above the grey sky
I know that I will find it
Yes, I will try

394

TRAUMA

THERE ARE TIMES WHEN THINGS FALL APART
MAYBE THIS IS ONE OF THOSE TIMES
DOOR LOCKED, CURTAINS DRAWN AGAINST THE SICKENING SKY
THE UNDENIABLE TRUTH EXPERIENCED IN CLOSE PROXIMITY
OH THE UNENVIABLE DUNCE
AND THE OBSERVER
ONE STEP, TWO STEPS REMOVED
HAD TO LAUGH
BUT STILL THE BRUISE ON THE WALL OF THE HEART
AND WHERE DO I SIT AS THINGS FALL APART?
AM I (LOWERCASE) IN THE MIDST OF THIS EXODUS
THINGS FROM THEIR RIGHTFUL PLACE?
I WAS BUT NOT TODAY
LET IT FALL
LET'S SEE THE WEAVE OF FABRICATION
BRING ON THE DISSIPATION
THE DISAPPEARING ACT
ALL RABBIT NO HAT
FACTS FLY IN THE FACE OF TRUTH
SWAT THEM AWAY
WIPE CLEAR THE CONDENSATION FROM THE BATHROOM MIRROR
YES, STILL REFLECTING
SO MUCH TIME SPENT
SPENT IT SQUANDERED
SELF-ABSORBED
CHEWED OVER FRAGMENTS
FEELINGS, OF ALL THE USELESS
I'LL FIND THE LIGHT BETWEEN THE CRACKS
I WON'T TOLERATE ANYTHING LESS
BLOW IT TO SMITHEREENS
THERE IS NO PERIPHERY
ONLY CANDIED CENTER
DUB REALITY
RIFFS ON A SYLLABLE
MUTE NOISE
I'LL BLOW YOU AWAY
BIG GUNS BLAZING
LAST MAN STANDING
YOU AND WHOSE ARMY?
I'LL BLOW YOU AWAY

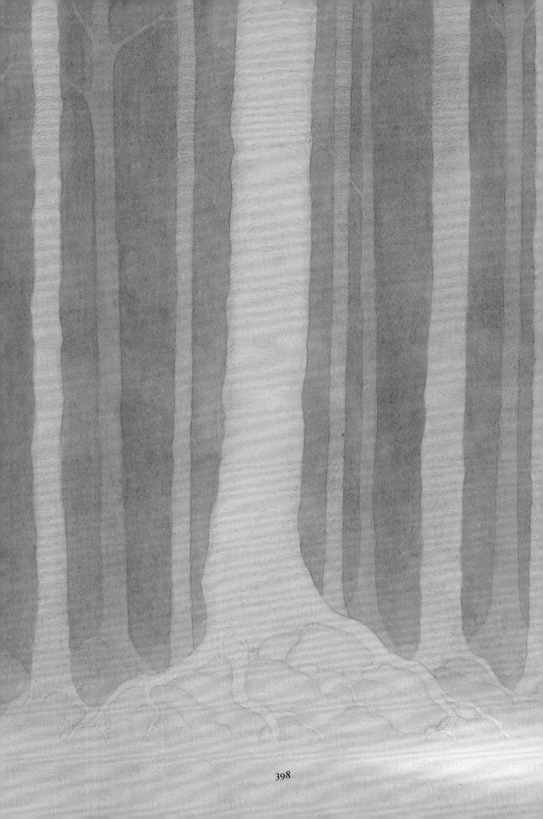

WASN'T I JOE?

Don't stay away too long love
I sense there's something wrong
Don't stay away too long love
Don't stay away too long

And the minutes last a lifetime
They've mastered ways of moving slow
She took the children and the cheque book
Should I have really let her go?

Don't stay away too long love
Don't stay away too long

There's a moving recitation
Played out inside my head
With an eloquence I don't possess
I think it's better left unsaid

Where's the examples that we needed
A man and wife that walk the line?
Give me something to aspire to
Not in our lifetime, not in our life

Don't stay away too long love
I know that something's wrong
There's a sadness I can't live with
Don't stay away too long

Today's the day before I met her
Now these things pass unrecognised
These are the shoes, that was the workplace
And this the car in which we cried

So many hours of conversation
I doubt there's anything left unsaid
The hope of reconciliation
Slowly paces round my bed

And the walls echo disturbance
They're screaming from the inside too
You left with everything we lived for
The everything of me and you

I was strong myself when I started
Wasn't I Joe?

Black lines run throughout the notebooks
A life in letters scribbled out
There's no place left now for reflection
We're not leaving room for doubt

I've got you pictured in my mind love
You're off the bus and running free
I'll keep the memories and the pretence
The ghosts of who we used to be

And I'll be nothing like my father
We'll wash the sheets as if by hand
And you'll be nothing like my mother
We're abandoning the plan

Aren't we Joe?

Wasn't I Joe?

And sometimes life is frightening
And everything comes on strong
So we're holding on for dear life
'Til something better comes along

'Til something better comes along

EXIT/DELETE

Feels like an ending
She's winding her way towards a conclusion
That never comes
Caroline feels uncomfortably numb

She's in deep
Surrendering to the promise of sleep
Almost done
Caroline plays an audience of one

And it isn't polite
She won't even try
A problem to no one
A problem to none

How can it be as quiet as this
This close to the edge?
Caroline says she's nobody's friend

How can you breathe
Embarrassed to be this far left of alone?
Caroline knows there's nobody home

It's ending
Winding its way towards a conclusion
Nearly done
Caroline knows there's nothing to come

When in doubt
She wanted to get it all down in writing
Didn't count
Better if someone else works it out

The files are deleted
No resisting at all
Already defeated

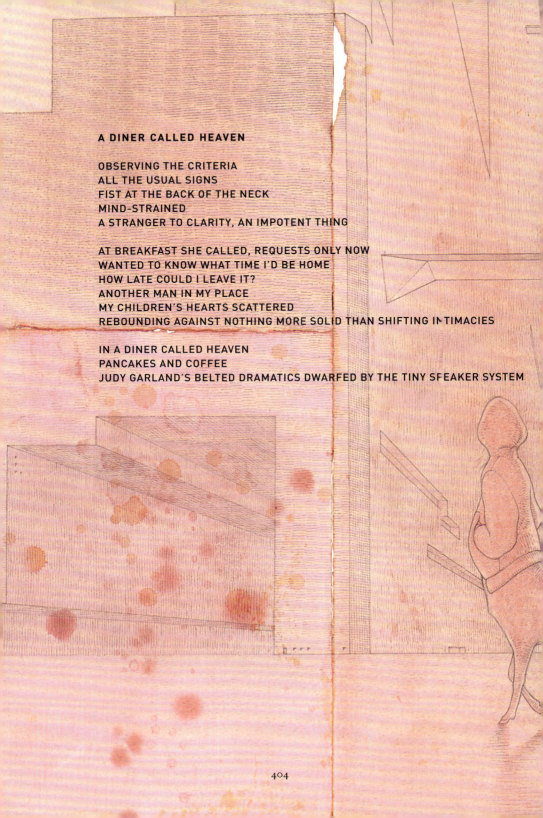

A DINER CALLED HEAVEN

OBSERVING THE CRITERIA
ALL THE USUAL SIGNS
FIST AT THE BACK OF THE NECK
MIND-STRAINED
A STRANGER TO CLARITY, AN IMPOTENT THING

AT BREAKFAST SHE CALLED, REQUESTS ONLY NOW
WANTED TO KNOW WHAT TIME I'D BE HOME
HOW LATE COULD I LEAVE IT?
ANOTHER MAN IN MY PLACE
MY CHILDREN'S HEARTS SCATTERED
REBOUNDING AGAINST NOTHING MORE SOLID THAN SHIFTING INTIMACIES

IN A DINER CALLED HEAVEN
PANCAKES AND COFFEE
JUDY GARLAND'S BELTED DRAMATICS DWARFED BY THE TINY SPEAKER SYSTEM

"GOD HELP ME, GOD HELP ME"
AN ELDERLY LADY AT THE COUNTER SEIZED BY A FIT OF SNEEZING
NECK LODGED AT RIGHT ANGLES TO HER BODY HIT BY TREMOR AFTER TREMOR
HER MANTRA REPEATED WITH WEARY RESIGNATION
THE PLACE IS EMPTYING OUT
SUNDAY MORNING RUSH IS OVER
THE BLACK WAITRESS (ONE IS TEMPTED TO SAY "NEGRO") AN APPARITION
PARTIALLY ERADICATED
SHE WALKS AT A PACE PRACTICED BY MONKS
BUT RE-SHUFFLED, MADE HER OWN.
RAKE THIN, BEAUTIFUL BONES OF ENORMOUS FRAGILITY
HARD NOT TO ADMIRE THE EFFORT OF WILL SUMMONED TO PLOUGH ON
MY AGE? OLDER, THOUGH HARD TO TELL
CLOTHING WELL CARED FOR
CRISP WHITES, IMPENETRABLE BLACKS
LINT FREE
HISTORY WORN ON THE SURFACE
PERVASIVE AS PERFUME
IF I CONCENTRATE HARD ENOUGH I'LL ABSORB
ALL THERE IS TO KNOW ABOUT HER
I FILL WITH AN IMPROBABLE AFFECTION

HER PRESENCE IN THE MOMENT LACKS CONVICTION
THE RESULT OF SOME TERRIBLE COMPROMISE WITH THE PAST
SHE'S SURVIVED WHATEVER ONCE THREATENED TO ERASE HER
THE PRESENT PROPELLING HER FORWARDS DESPITE THE ANCHOR OF MEMORY
IF WE COULD WILL THE HEART TO IMMOBILITY
HOW MANY LEFT STANDING?

SECOND WAVE, PANCAKES COFFEE OR TEA
I WONDER, IS IT POSSIBLE
TO LOVE SOMEONE WHO DOESN'T KNOW SORROW?

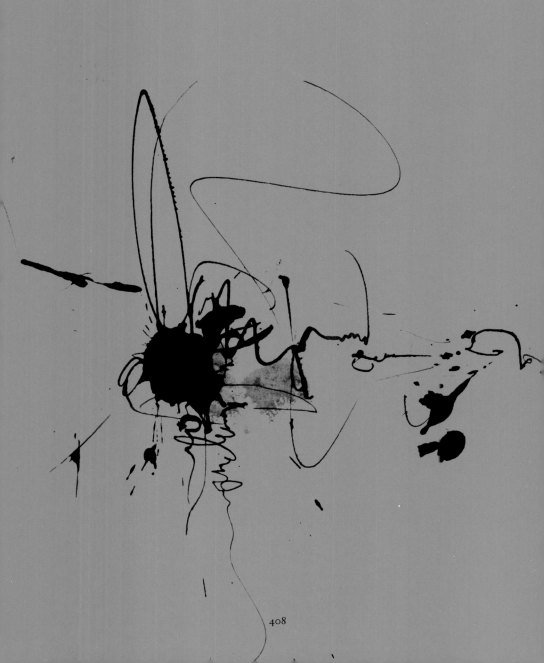

03/06 - SNOW BORNE SORROW

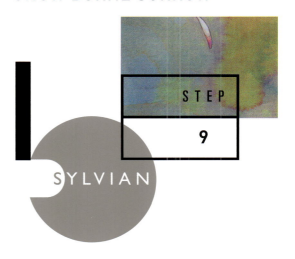

STEP

9

SYLVIAN

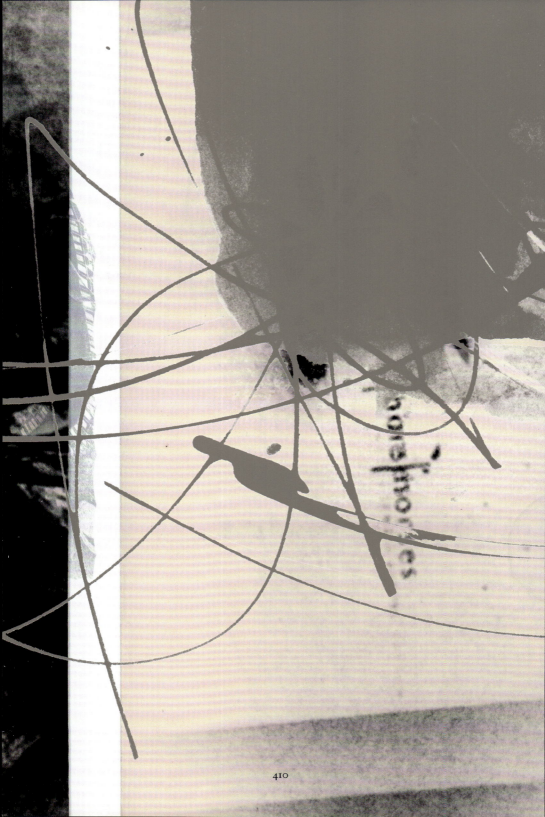

SNOW BORNE SORROW

nine/horse

WONDERFUL WORLD

It's a wonderful world
And you take and you give
And the sun fills the sky
In the space where you live

It's a day full of dreams
It's a dream of a day
And the joy that it brings
Nearly sweeps her away

It's a wonderful world
As the buildings fall down
And you quicken your step
'Til your feet leave the ground
And you're soaring above
All the sorrow below
And you're falling in love
With those you don't know

And your heart feels so wide
And your heart fills so strong
It was never a place
That you felt you belonged

It's a wonderful world
Full of wonderful things
And the people fall down
And abandon their dreams

(I hear him, he's talking out loud
Sometimes he whistles while walking
How could he know any better?
I weep for him, I weep for him now)

It's a wonderful world
It's a real crying shame
'Cause she's hurting herself
In a violent way
And there's people she knows
That won't even try
And they're trapped in their lives
Feeling terrified

And it's in times like these
That she promised to call
But the scale of our love
Is diminished and small

It's a wonderful world
And she doesn't know why
She wakes up each day
And continues to cry

(He's sleeping his troubles away
He's finding it too hard to bear
I'm with him every step of the way
I weep for him, I weep for him now)

It's a wonderful world
And you take and you give
And the sun fills the sky
In the space where you live

DARKEST BIRDS

Here come the darkest birds
To burst the bubble
End of a perfect day
Head full of trouble

Here come the darkest birds
All tar and feathers
Why did none of them dream of trying
To make things better?

Those are the mimicking kind
They are, they are
I number myself among them
The furthest star

And this is the road I walked on
When I shot you down
All words of forgiveness useless
They won't help me now
And I should've been there for you
When you called my name
I promise to tread more lightly
Though what's gone is gone
It's such a shame

Here come the darkest birds
They've got their reasons
All their pretty colours are gone
Washed out of season

Those are the soaring kind
They are, they are
I number yourself among them
The brightest star

And this is the road I walked on
When I shot you down
All words of forgiveness useless
They won't serve me now
And I should've been there for you
When you called my name
I promise to tread more lightly
Though what's done is done
It's such a shame

THE BANALITY OF EVIL

I got me a badge
A bright shiny badge
I'm painting the crest in yellow and blue

I've got me a club
An exclusive club
It doesn't include a place for you

Hey, hello neighbour
Hey, hello neighbour, right you are

It's in the way that you walk
All of the changes, all the mistakes
It's in the demands you constantly make

It's in the way that you grieve
All of the loss
You don't know when you're better off
Or at what cost
You've got it good

The banality of evil

Benevolent mother
Smother the child
The benefactors are in denial

Hey, hello neighbour
Hey, hello neighbour, right you are

There was a time
Not so long ago
I was master of everything I surveyed
Yes, there was a time
We did it my way
We'll do things my way

Benevolent mother
Smother the child
The perpetrators are in denia

The banality of evil

King of the castle
Room at the top
Off with their heads
Chop 'em off

The banality of evil

Benevolent mother
Smother the child
The benefactors are in denial

420

The banality of evil   Hey, hello neighbour

King of the castle   Benevolent mother
Room at the top   Smother the child
Off with their heads   The benefactors are in denial
Chop 'em off

    The banality of evil

Hey, hello neighbour

    King of the castle
I don't believe in what you believe   Room at the top
Your skin is filthy   Off with their heads
And your gods don't look like God to me   Chop 'em off

But I want to touch you   The banality of evil
Now that isn't right
No, that can't be right   Benevolent mother
But I want to touch you   Smother the child
You're leading me on I know it   The perpetrators are in denial

Hey...   The banality of evil

King of the castle   King of the castle
More room at the top   Room at the top
All sorts allowed   Off with their heads
Now the gloves are off   Chop 'em off

    The banality of evil

ATOM AND CELL

Her skin was darker than ashes
And she had something to say
'Bout being naked to the elements
At the end of yet another day
And the rain on her back that continued to fall
From the bruise of her lips
Swollen, fragile, and small

And the bills that you paid with were worth nothing at all
A lost foreign currency
Multi-coloured, barely reputable
Like the grasses that blew in the warm summer breeze
Well she offered you this to do as you pleased

And where is the poetry
Didn't she promise us poetry?

The redwoods, the deserts, the tropical ease
The swamps and the prairie dogs, the Joshua trees
The long straight highways from dirt road to tar
Hitching your wheels to truck, bus, or car

And the lives that you hold in the palm of your hand
You toss them aside small and damn near unbreakable
You drank all the water and you pissed yourself dry
Then you fell to your knees and proceeded to cry

And who could feel sorry for a drunkard like this
In a democracy of dunces with a parasite's kiss?

And where are the stars
Didn't she promise us stars?

Nothing will ever be as it was
The price has been paid with a thousand loose shoes
Pictures are pasted on shop windows and walls
Like a poor man's Boltanski
Lost one and all.

Sell, sell
Bid your farewell
Come, come
Save yourself
Give yourself over
Pushing your consciousness
Deep into every atom and cell,
Sell,
Bid your farewell
Come, come
Save yourself
Give yourself over
Pushing your consciousness
Deep into every atom and cell,
Sell,
Bid your farewell
Come, come
Save yourself
Give yourself over
Pushing your consciousness
Deep into every atom and cell

A HISTORY OF HOLES

I'm having my day
My place in the sun
I'll grow to resemble
The man I've become

There'll be time for reflection
When I reach that plateau
When the war has been won
No farther to go

And I fear that it isn't enough

I'm making a fortune
I swore to enjoy
These things I promised myself
When I was a boy

When I was a boy
And things moved too slow
And universes revolved around
Things I didn't know

When I was a boy
And I made mistakes
I was humiliated
'Til I knew my place

And I fear that it isn't enough

Ignorance hurts
Injustice inflames
I remember the feelings
But forgotten their names

When I was a boy
I saw through their lies
I swore I wouldn't become
The thing I despised
But events overtake you
While you set your sights
On bigger game
On greater heights

God bless amnesia
And the things I've suppressed
I can reframe the image
I can discard the rest

A history of holes
Where the pieces won't fit
With the story you told yourself
And your place in it

So put on a brave face
Straighten that tie
And speak like you mean it
Give truth to the lie

And I fear that it isn't enough

SNOW BORNE SORROW

Strip the branches
Unsheathe the hatchets
The threads of friendship
Are coming off

With the knives drawn apart
They shatter the heart
Of anyone that dares come between them

Let the children come to me

The teeth of lawyers
Man the trenches
Bands of betrothal
Are coming off

Once a playground of swings
Then the malice set in
And reduced all the colours to winter

But if we're good, if we're kind
But if we're good, generous and kind
We'll inhabit their sunsets
Their goddesses and queens
We'll try to do the right thing

So we made it our own
This snow borne sorrow
And this love that stutters and splinters

Let the children come to me

(Oh save them)
Oh save them
(Oh save them)
(Oh save them)
Oh save them
(Oh save them)

Her apostles have gone
They left one by one
With no forwarding address to trace them

It's a secular world
Of adults and girls
And we ask because nothing is certain

Let the children come to me

Let the children come to me

It's a harrowing world
Of adults and girls
Lashing out at the hurt
That surrounds them

When their feet touch the ground
Naked unbound
I want them to know they can trust me

There's so much to be ungrateful for

Let the children come to me

THE DAY THE EARTH STOLE HEAVEN

Let me tell you about a friend
She contends she will always love me

It's this ability to lie and deceive
That has lost me completely

I could remind her of the facts
Make her calm down and relax
But why bother?

It's the shallowest defense
To my utter astonishment it is over

That little girl she wants to leave me
That little girl wants something more.

I'm optimistically inclined
Given time she'll change her mind
It's unlikely

Let me tell you about a friend
She contends she will always love me

If you look at her sideways
She will let you know

Today's the day the earth stole heaven

If you look at her sideways
She will curse you out

Today's the day the earth stole heaven

If you look at her sideways
There can be no doubt
It's over

SEROTONIN

I kick the sheets
Until they rise like mountain ranges at my feet

I'm in the dark
God only knows the torment writ large upon my
heart

What wouldn't I
What wouldn't I give?

It comes to this
I'm only sure of things I know now don't exist

There's no precision
I'm inside-outside-in
I want subdivision

And all of this fills my aching head
I hate this space, the luxury hotel bed
Oh dear, oh me-oh-my
Got to concentrate just to keep from trying
Oh dear, oh me-oh-my
Got to concentrate just to keep from trying
Don't lose it
Things move rapidly
Don't lose it
Try to maintain composure
Don't lose it
The dead are haunting me
Out with it
Out with it, let's get it over

What wouldn't I
What wouldn't I give?

I'm thoroughly wasted
My mind's hallucinating lucidity

It's over sensitised
And something's moving on the periphery

What wouldn't I
What wouldn't I give?

THE LIBRARIAN

Keep your head down
Keep your head down
While they're firing low
You're too young child
To know the difference

Oh my pretty
Oh my sweet girl
It's a marvelous place
They put weights down
In your coattails to burn you out

Lest you fly
Lest you take off
And show whomever what's what
It's one outrageous lie after another

Turn their lights out
Change the channel
Before we lose the heart
To fight against belief in what they're saying

There's a hotel
With a dark room
At the end of a corridor
I will meet you
To the strains of Allah

We will lie back
On a pillow of the whitest snow
And the silence we were promised
Will engulf us

Lay your head down
Keep your head down
While they're firing low
You're too young child
You're too young child

We will wake up
From the dreams that bury us
We will tunnel our way out
By moonlight

From the dark room
To the white streets and the snow
banks
We'll invest in one another's future

Oh my pretty
Oh my sweet girl
It's a marvelous place
She designed it
With escape routes
For you and me

So to the library
With a new card
Grab your favourite books
Look for blueprints
To the strains of Allah
Here we go...

Benevolence is in back
Of everyplace you look
It's not a monstrous face she is hiding

If I see her
I will tell you
You'll come quickly
If you see her
Don't hesitate just go

But 'til then

Keep your head down
Keep your head down
While they're firing low
You're too young child
You're too young child

You're too young child
Here we go....

TRANSIT

I have listened repeatedly
I have listened very well
No one interrupts the harmful when they're speaking

To wonder why of Europe
Say your goodbyes to Europe
Swallow the lie of Europe
Our shared history dies with Europe

(follow me, won't you follow me?)

A future's hinting at itself
Do you fear what I fear?
All those names of ancestry
Too gentle for the stones they bear

Somewhere someone wants to see you
Someone's traveling towards us all

To wonder why of Europe
To live, love, and cry in Europe
Say your goodbyes to Europe
Our history dies with Europe

(follow me, won't you follow me?)

The lights are dimming, the lounge is dark
The best cigarette is saved for last
We drink alone
We drink alone

ANGELS

High in the architecture
Something's moving
Unrecognisable spirit
Dislocated
It's the wrong climate
No humidity
Humming humidity

Its face belongs to another time
Another place

Projections on falling masonry
Ghosts of a once pagan place
Stand empty

I stand empty

Dead echo
Dead echoes don't come back
It's stopped, cut out, (fuck you)
Nothing ever happens
Unbelieving, no one's receiving
A vessel filled, held, and spilled

Nothing

A trace from another time
Another place

It's simple
You don't exist
Can't possess me
You lose on a technicality

High in the architecture
Something's moving

Nothing

FOR THE LOVE OF LIFE

And slowly you come to realise
It's all as it should be
You can only do so much

If you're game enough
You could place your trust in me

For the love of life
There's a trade off
We could lose it all
But we'll go down fighting

And what of the children
Surely they can't be blamed
For our mistakes?

And slowly I've come to realise
It's all as it should be

That hiding space
A lonely place

How can the right thing be so wrong?
I've found mistakes where they don't belong

For the love of life
We'll defeat this
They may tear us down
But we'll go down fighting

Won't we?

PURE GENIUS

Oh, the lights are blinking
Here's the great deceiver
Bling bling, all bets are off
It goes unnoticed
If not for me it goes unnoticed

Find another record
Play another record
It could be anything
I play the jukebox
I play the DJ
I could be vice, FBI
I played the imbecile
And no one noticed
And no one noticed

Oh boy, come see the plans
They're pure genius
Pure genius
Oh boy, come see the plans...

Oh, you wouldn't notice
Here they come
See them tumble
My lucky numbers
Here they come
I've got lots of secrets
Man, I've lots of secrets
And you're my number one
And you're my number one

So, I fill the notebooks
Yeah, they fill the room
I've got the meaning
I think I've worked it out
Yes, it's all in neon
It's in the details
Click/flash, I think it's coming back
I think the wheels are turning

Oh boy, come see the plans
They're pure genius
Pure genius
Oh boy, get with the program man
Come see the plans
They're pure genius
You understand, you understand

Oh, the lights are blinking
Turn off the stereo
It wears the batteries
They're double As

Come morning
I'll sleep like a dog
And dream of numbers
My lucky numbers

Here they come

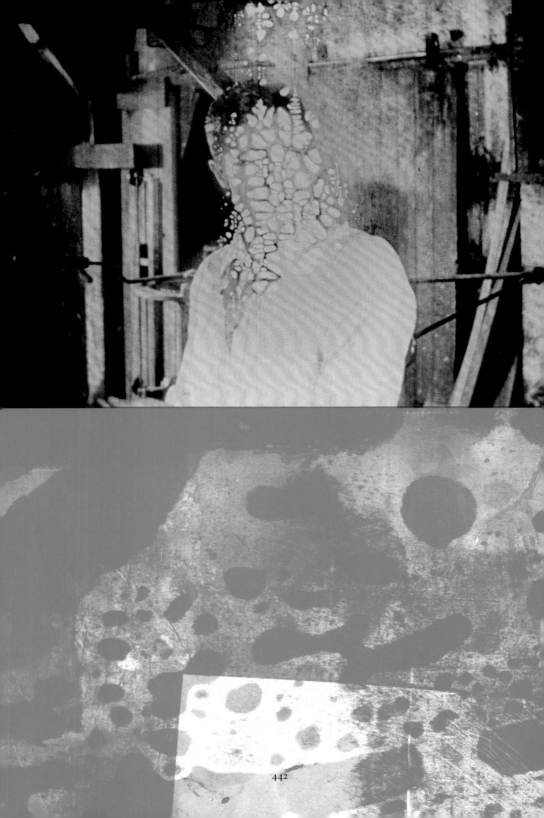

442

BALLAD OF A DEADMAN

Oh honey take me out I'm a deadman
Oh baby bake me something sweet
Oh honey take me out I'm a deadman
Oh baby give me bread to eat

There are places in the damp Northwest where
The bodies lie down head to feet
There were losses in the California sunshine
Tell you stories that you can't repeat

In the Winter when the valleys flooded
Those were towns where the rooms were cheap
The summer dirt lines the corners of your pockets
I'm still buried there ten feet deep

Papa don't place this curse on me
Heaven knows I can't use it
Papa don't place this stone on me
Mama there's no future in it.

We travel on the back roads lightly
Through Carson City and the hills beyond
Me and Joan on the Sacramento
Me and Joan this is where we're from

Oh honey take me out I'm a deadman
Oh baby bake me something sweet
Oh honey take me out I'm a deadman
Oh baby give me bread to eat

Papa don't place this curse on me
Heaven knows I can't use it
Papa don't place this curse on me
Mama there's no future in it.

Oh honey take me out I'm a deadman
Oh baby bake me something sweet
Oh honey take me out I'm a deadman
Oh baby give me bread to eat

Oh honey wears the colours of the Springtime
The pale green of an organdy dress
Her shadow grows in the California sunshine
But nothing else in the South, Southwest.

(for joan didion)

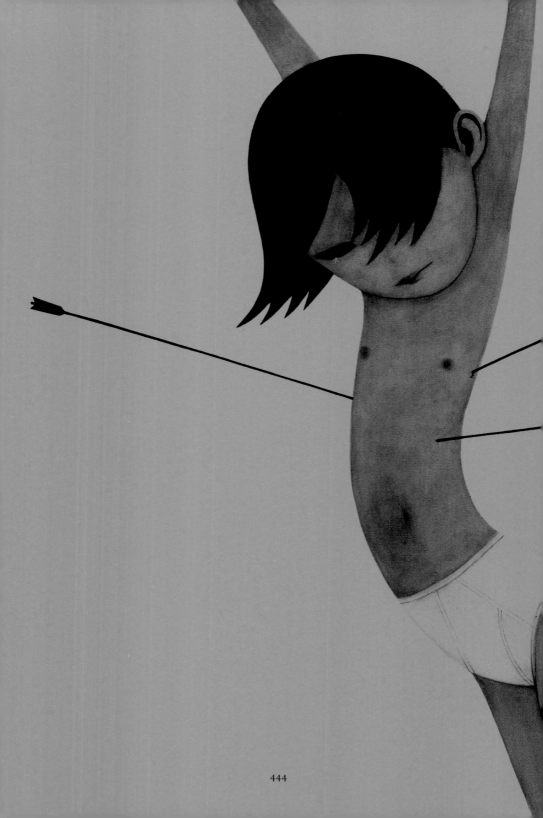

PLAYGROUND MARTYRS

You run to the gate but you'll be marked late
It's for your own good, it's for your own good

You're likely to make the grandest mistakes
You suffer alone in the skin and the bone

Let's sharpen those new sets of arrows
For the next generation of playground martyrs
And join in the game of intolerable shame
'Cause everyone shares in the sins of their fathers

School bell rings, single-file in
Trade you my unhappily ever-afters
So bring out the things to hammer the wings
Of the next generation of playground martyrs

MONEY FOR ALL

Wanna step on through?   All change
Can I check that bag?   All change
Is there something inside here   Let gasoline fumes fill the air
That could help you relax?   Let's show that mother how much you care

Did you find something   All change
You were looking for?   All change
Freedom has its price now   Wipe your nation's shame from you
Wanna buy some more?   It's not where you're born
   It's the things that you do

I'll take the coat
Remove them shoes   Money for all
Should a guy like me be afraid
Of a man like you?   Money for all

All change, all change   Hey there soldier
Wipe your nation's shame from you   Who's your concubine?
It's not where you're born   With her trigger-happy finger
It's the things that you do   And her nicotine friend
   She's a diamond mine

Money for all
Money for all   All change
Revolution's socialism   All change
Read it in the rag   Let revolution fill the air
There's a gun at your head   Let's show that monkey how much you care
Put the money in the bag
Money for all   Money for all
   There's a mean looking elephant
Have you tried this game   Pounding on your door
When you're feeling tired?   It's dining at your table
Keeps you entertained   Sleeping on your floor
'Til your card expires   Money for all
   Money for all
So you missed the broadcast   Revolution's socialism
But do you feel the same?   Read it in the rag
Only someone said that city's gone   There's a gun at your head
Down in flames in our name   Put the money in the bag

GET THE HELL OUT

Get the hell out
Honey it's your birthday
Get the hell out
Honey it's your birthday

Check the phonebook
Find a close relation
Pack a suitcase
Get ye to the station

Get the hell out
Honey it's your birthday
Find a motel
Book yourself a long stay

Find a safe house
Far from this location
Take some good advice
Get ye to the station

When he finds out
You know you've got it coming
If you survive this
Girl you're really something

Get the hell out

Caroline, you're breaking my heart
But I remain unchanged
Get the hell out
(threaten me, threaten me)
Caroline, Caroline, you're breaking my heart
But I remain unchanged

Get the hell out

Caroline, you're breaking my heart
But I remain unchanged
And yours, yours was the saddest face
I would never, you know, I would never...
Caroline, Caroline, I would never...

Get the hell out

452

WHEN MONDAY COMES AROUND

The letters I write, I write for you
But they're not easy
And the words I used, I made mistakes
There's no explaining
Where is the excuse
For the things we said and the things we left unsaid?
Believe me, I know, I know
Now the game is up
And there'll be no stopping you from leaving
Oh God, oh no

When Monday comes around
I'll be waiting
When Monday comes around
I'll be waiting
When Monday comes around
I'll be losing you and I'll be breaking

They forecast snow
And where are you this evening?
And chances are the snow won't fall
But I want it outside me as in
Where the colour's gone
And your footprints mark the space you're leaving
I know you know
And the weather was always your best friend
You're needed, don't go, don't go

When Monday comes around
I'll be waiting
When Monday comes around
I'll be waiting
When Monday comes around
I'll be losing you and I'll be breaking

JACQUELINE

The big man came and took the sun away
And replaced it with one of his own
There was no room for sharing
Just nurse and care for him
Fill his shoes with concrete and stone

Oh, Jacqueline, Jacqueline
Things are getting harder
There's only now 'til the end and nothing in-between

Keep his children from his door
Protect the one that you waited for
You can't breathe when his eyes aren't on you
Though you may feel the bite of his tongue
The back of his hand, you're not the only one
And it's his and he alone will do

Oh, Jacqueline, Jacqueline
Things are getting harder
There's only now 'til the end and nothing in-between

And when you wake, you wake to the same day
The one where your Mediterranean sky turned grey
And you withdrew into the shadow of you
And while asleep you'd lose his name
And the footsteps of one defiantly sound the same
So you bolted the bathroom door and flew

Oh, Jacqueline, Jacqueline
Things can't get much harder
Only now it's the end

THE WORLD IS EVERYTHING

The world is everything

The world is everything

And I move close
But you move closer
And out of the Spring
And into the Summer
And out of the dark
Into the blessing of others

The table of goods
The bright bolt of lightning
And she loved him there once
But she's still not through fighting

And you can't swallow it
But you can't spit it out
It's there in her hair
It's coming out of her eyes
To taste her is bitter
But the world is alive

And the world is everything
The world is everything
The world is everything
The world is everything

UNCOMMON DEITIES

MAYBE THIS IS THE ROOM IN WHICH IT STARTED
A PLACE OF NURTURE AND WITHDRAWAL
AND THE DIVISION OF SKIN
BETWEEN INTERIOR AND EX.
BREACHED
SELF INVADING THE SPACE OF NON-SELF
THE FOUNDATION OF FOUR-WALLED
REALITY DEMATERIALISED
SCALE AND DIMENSION LOST IN A
POP-TARKOVSKY DREAM STATE

AND MUSIC... FOREVER

HALLUCINOGENIC LANDSCAPES RESEMBLE
NASA SHOTS OF DISTANT COSMOS
IRRADIATED COLOUR
THE MUTANT VEGETATION A PRIMORDIAL PRESENCE
REPRESENTATIVES OF A PERVASIVE CONSCIOUSNESS
UNCOMMON DEITIES

AMBIENT MANGA
CHARACTERS CUT OFF, CAST ADRIFT
ABSENTED FROM STORY LINE
SUNK IN AMBIVALENT SELF ABSORPTION
BACKGROUND MAGNIFIED
THEY HAUNT THEIR EMOTIONAL LANDSCAPES

A TEENAGE SELF CONTAINMENT
THAT COMFORT OF MELANCHOLY
A LOOSE LIMBED SENSUALITY
PERMEATES THE FOREST

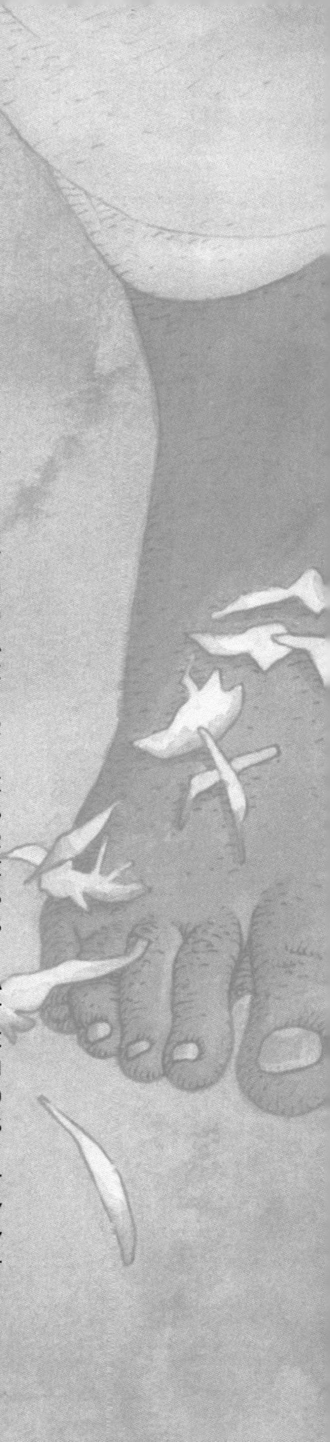

ARCHETYPAL MESSENGERS IN PLAIN VIEW
NAVIGATORS OF THE DREAM REALITY
SHAMANIC PATHFINDERS
THEIR FOOTFALLS THE ONLY CERTAINTY
AN IMMATERIAL TRUTH

YES, INSIDE'S OUT
AN ENERGY SOURCED FROM
INEXHAUSTIBLE CIRCUITRY
PLUGGED IN, LIFE RADIATES FROM WALL SOCKETS
WITH DIVINE LUMINESCENCE
AND THE RURAL IN CONTRAST HAS ALL
THE HYGIENE OF AN APPLIANCE STORE
ALIENATION EXUDES A SENSE OF COMFORT
BORROWED FROM ITS ORIGINS IN THE HOME

SIXTIES PSYCHEDELIC POSTER ART
IN MEDIA OF DUST MOTES AND LIGHT PARTICLES
A FINE SHERBET POWDER POP PATINA
BAKER'S GLAZE, SOUL CANDY

ON THE THRESHOLD OF THE
COURTYARD AT THE CITY'S EXTREMITY
AS TRUTH AND IDENTITY BECOME
INCREASINGLY MALLEABLE
WITH NO FIXED POINTS OF REFERENCE
HE LEAVES THE DOOR AJAR
AN INVITATION FOR THE RETURN OF THE CELESTIAL

(for atsushi fukui)

464

BEFORE AND AFTERLIFE

WE STARTED IN THE SUBURBS OF SMALLER CITIES
AND AS WE FOLLOWED THE NOMADIC CALL
OUR NOBLER INSTINCTS LED US FURTHER FROM
SOCIETY'S CENTER, WESTWARD, TO A CABIN HOISTED
ALOFT ON FAULTY FOUNDATIONS FAR ABOVE THE NAPA VALLEY
WHERE THE RAIN SOAKED EARTH SHIFTED BENEATH US AND TREES CAUGHT
LIKE KINDLING, SMOKE CLOUDS RIPENING
A VINTNER'S SUN
BUT PART OF US REFUSED TO FOLLOW
MATERIAL DISTRACTIONS BECKONED, RALLIED
SNAGGED, WE'D RETURN TO THE CITIES ON DAY TRIPS AND LONG WEEKENDS
SELF-AVERSION, ANONYMITY FOUND ONLY IN
THE MIDST OF BRICKS AND MORTAR, THE
HUSTLE OF STRANGERS
WE WERE WORLDLY PEOPLE AFTER ALL
BUT THE HAZE OF THE RURAL, THE AGENTS OF POLLINATION,
CLUNG TO US, SPARKED LIKE HAYSEED HALOS IN THE WESTERN SUNLIGHT
NO ONE LET ON THEY'D NOTICED
BUT WE SAW, WE KNEW

   I WATCHED MY PARENTS AS THEY STOOD IN A CROWDED EUSTON STATION

   UP FRESH FROM THE COUNTRY, SUITCASES AT THEIR SIDES

   WAITING ON MY ARRIVAL, ILLUMINATED

   IN AN OTHERWISE SEA OF GREY

   NOT OF THIS WORLD

WE WERE TEMPTED BACK REPEATEDLY
UNTIL THE LURE OF THE COSMOPOLITAN
LAY BEYOND REACH
WE MOVED EAST, INTO THE FORESTS AND MOUNTAINS
WHERE LIFE'S DESIRES TORE US APART
HOW CRUEL TO FIND ONESELF ALONE AT THAT ALTITUDE
AT WHAT POINT DID THE FEAR OF NUMBERS SET IN
AND THE RECOGNITION OF INTERNAL ISOLATION PLACE US OUTSIDE OF BELONGING?
BUT THEN WASN'T THAT ALWAYS THE CASE, WEREN'T WE SIMPLY
ALLOWED TO FORGET?
ON TEMPLE MOUNTAIN I THREW DOWN A ROPE THAT OTHERS MIGHT FOLLOW
NO ONE CAME

THERMAL

MORNING, YOU LAY SLEEPING
YOUR SMALL BODY CLINGING TIGHTLY TO MINE
WITH FRIGHTENING DEPENDENCY
LIFE DEFINING, IMPOSSIBLE TO BETRAY

AND WITH THAT...
THE MATTRESS ROSE
SET ADRIFT ON THE BURGEONING EMOTIONAL TIDE
COLLIDING WITH THE ONCE STATIONARY OBJECTS
OF AN UNINHABITED LIFE

WHAT HAD BEEN CONCEALED
WAS EXHALED FROM GOD KNOWS WHERE
COLOUR-DRAINED, UNSALVAGEABLE
SHAPE SHIFTING
AND, WITH FUNCTION RELINQUISHED
RESIGNED FROM SERVICE

TWO BLUE SLEEPING BAGS
NUDGED AGAINST ONE ANOTHER
BEARING THE ONCE WARM IMPRINT OF OUR BODIES

THE SUN-BAKED STONE GARDEN
RETRACTED ITS PROMISE
IT WAS COLD IN THAT PLACE OF PERPETUAL SUMMER

IF YOU WERE AFRAID YOU DIDN'T SHOW IT
YOU WHO WERE BORN BEARING THE FACE
OF IRREPRESSIBLE GRIEF

SO AS NOT TO DISAPPOINT YOU
I LAY MOTIONLESS
RAPT BY THE RISE AND STALL OF YOUR BREATHING
YOUR FINGERTIPS AND THIGHS
QUIETLY AFFIRMING MY PLACE AT YOUR SIDE

IN HIS LIKENESS

AS A BOY ALONE IN HIS FATHER'S SHED
HE'D ATTACHED MOTHS TO COTTON THREAD AND ANCHORED
THE ENDS TO THE WORKBENCH SURFACE
BENEATH A NAKED SIXTY WATT BULB
THE FAITHFUL LIFTED, FLOCKING TOWARDS THE UNOBTAINABLE LIGHT
ALL THAT BLACK CLOTHED, DRY WINGED ASPIRATION WAS CAPTIVATING
THE STRENUOUS RISE AND FALL
THE ARRESTED ASCENSION
UNTIL EXHAUSTION LED TO A FLOUNDERING IN SHADOWS
A THIRSTY BATTING AGAINST TABLE LEGS

HE'D FILL HIS GLASS WITH SOMETHING SWEET
THIS BOY, NO STRANGER TO EMPATHY
AND DRINK IT IN
THE ACTIVITY CONTAINED BEAUTY BUT NO JOY
ONLY ITS OPPOSITE
IT PUT THINGS IN PERSPECTIVE

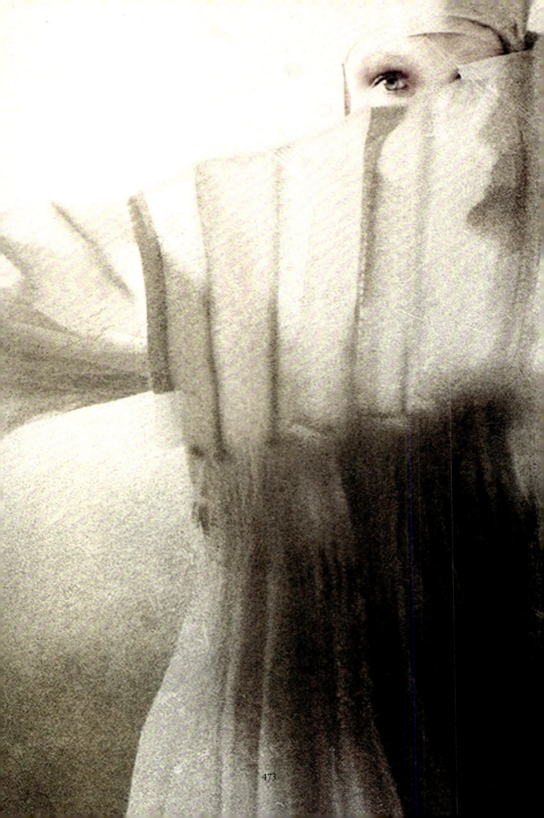

474

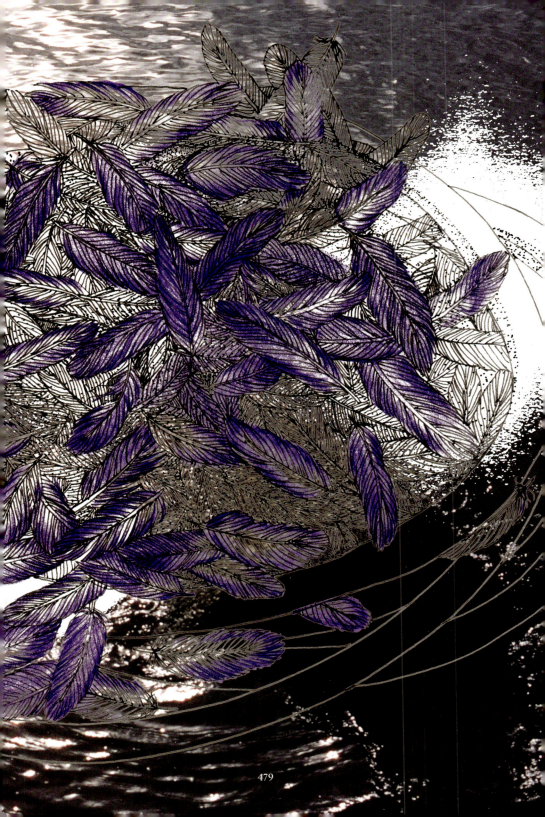

When Loud Weather Buffeted

Naoshima

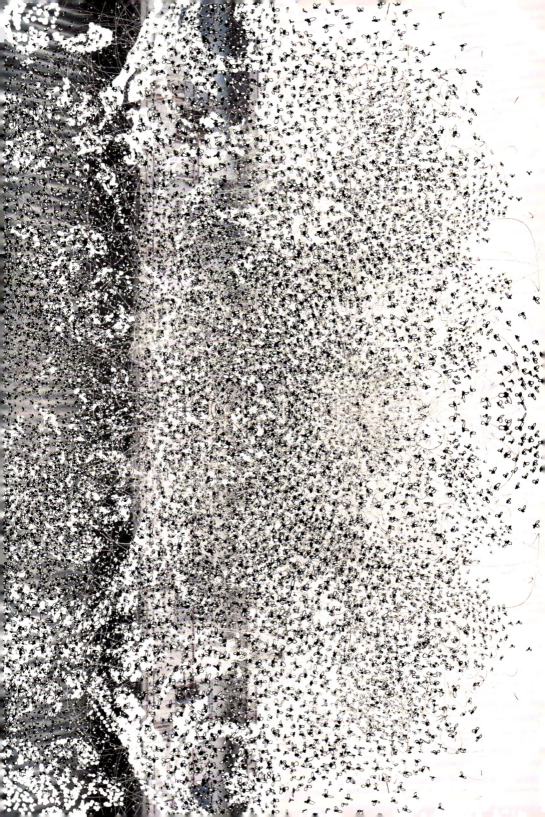

a conversation with

DAVID SYLVIAN

by NATALIA KUTSEPOVA

WITNESS AND PARTICIPANT

— **NK**: Your output seems to be a continuous exercise in sharpening the senses—your own and, by extension, those of your audience. A microscope, if you will, revealing a universe that's not there for the naked eye. You express yourself very strongly, but with incredible restraint, with subtle touches. This plenty in scarcity's clothing is a lifetime strategy of hiding, it seems. And at the same time hoping dearly that someone will hear and discover?

— **DS**: It's the best means I know how to communicate. Communication is an act of sharing. For it not to be heard, discovered, is for the work to remain incomplete, dormant. Restraint is something learned or acquired over time. The most powerful emotions are often uttered, if at all, by something muted, restrained, and in that restraint, in that enormous effort of restraint, so much is revealed. It's an ontological exercise I suppose, this tunneling at the roots of being. It's a subtle exercise conducted with inadequate equipment. A bulldozer with which to lift a needle. "...I, too, wish to make contact with some unknown person's inner life." (Charles Simic) We're capable of shorthand. We've seen so much played out through the history of our respective cultures. There are givens that need no longer be adhered to for the heart of the work to be communicated. We "read" the works we absorb as connoisseurs without being entirely aware of the fact that this is what we are or what it is we're doing. Sometimes a single word or image will suffice where there was once need for pages of explication or a series of set up shots etc. Poetry is particularly adept at working with the succinctly concise/precise. It could be argued that's part of its function. At a period in time, where the short attention span needs to get to the heart of the issue with a degree of rapidity, this condensation or act of compression seems all the more appropriate. I don't feel in any way protected or concealed by my work. On the contrary, as a result of all that's communicated there's a desire to save a little of myself for myself by leading a private life as far as that's possible. I can't recall who said it but I remember this line about the artist that fully exposes him/herself through their work, not simply standing naked but stripped to muscle, nervous system, bone, that in such instances, it's advisable to wear an all concealing cloak when in public for the sake of one's own sanity.

— **NK:** It's always a jigsaw—musician and his audience, his mindset and heartset and theirs. Who's first in your scheme? Where is the balance at the moment when music is created? How independent are you from those who (will) listen to you, and what is your reward when they do?

— **DS:** Without doubt it has to be total independence. You can't second guess what an audience will take to (okay, you can to a degree but that's cynical exploitation of which we see plenty). The point of the act is, as I said, to communicate something. The challenge is to find the most appropriate means with which to communicate in any particular instance. So you're true to what it is you're attempting to express. You're true to the needs of the composition and nothing else comes into play but how well that composition holds water, carries what it needs to communicate using the most efficient means possible. You've only yourself to gauge this fine balance between success and failure. "And a feeling of we're-right-here that you have to keep/Like carrying a pail filled to the brim without spilling a drop." (Tomas Tranströmer). You have to be present with the work until it reflects back to you the impetus for its creation. Then it's capable of standing alone. My reward for reaching the inner life of another human being? That's both intangible and incalculable. Much like an act of human kindness.

— **NK:** Was there, at any point in your life, an artist—a musician?—that affected you just as tangibly, as deeply as your own work affected some of your own listeners? Or are you, in this respect, "a water pipe that does not drink"?

— **DS:** It's impossible for me to know how my work affects those that hear it. There's no means of quantifying that impact. If I wasn't knocked off my feet by musicians, composers of all kinds, how could I find myself where I am now? It's essential to fall in love with aspects of a musician's output or a genre of music etc. Not one genre, one artist, but many, too many. But in later life... this is less necessary. Silence is often preferable.

— **NK:** A sort of transference—from the emotional impact of artistic work and onto the artist's personality—is incredibly common in the world of popular music. Was this ever an issue for you? Do you think it's in any way detrimental for those who experience it?

— **DS:** Even a listener that projects the emotional impact of the work onto the personality of the artist gets something out of the work that rewards their lives in some way so maybe all is not lost but very occasionally, yes, I think it can be detrimental to certain individuals that make that kind of transference, but in such instances you just happen to have become the focal point for forces already in play.

— **NK:** Much of what you did as pop artist was subterfuge—musical phrases too convoluted, modulations too unexpected, moments of atonality, lyrics ambiguous if not disturbing. Until "Blemish", the experiments remained subtle: the sound itself, the instrumentation, and the skeleton of a pop song proved a comfort enough to keep the listeners listening. By now, do you feel like you have sabotaged enough of pop-ness to be ousted into the "obscure experimenter" category? Would you say that perfection of form, which, to many, seemed to be your mission, was just a disguise all along?

— **DS:** The form was flexible and ample enough for the content. Or the content could be modified to sit comfortably within the form. Then suddenly the form was no longer a viable vessel. The content expanded, exploded, outgrew the form. It was therefore necessary to reinvent the form, or expand upon it, or to find forms of a more modular nature or invent new ones. I would still describe myself as a pop musician. The term is flexible, expansive and inclusive. If I was to describe myself as an "obscure experimenter" I would no doubt upset an altogether different category of people who would argue I've not pushed the envelope enough but it'd be an ill fitting description of what it is I'm up to regardless. Best to understand something of your musical roots, where it is you've come from, and view the resulting material as an offshoot from that particular branch of the tree even though there's been plenty of cross pollination along the way. What I'm currently producing isn't purposefully/willfully obscure. My intention is quite the opposite. The need for experimentation should be present in all forms of the arts, no? Are we happy with stasis in any of our art forms?

In popular music there is a point at which a long-term artist is notified that further experimentation isn't welcome. That a return to a career's highlights in terms of style and content would be advisable. This is indicated by a drop in sales and the threat of obscurity or, worse, irrelevance. Hence the constant bowing to the demands of the market which is fair enough. Not allowing the work to mature as the individual does is often seen as an act of complacency, cowardice, or a reflection of "Peter Pan syndrome" perhaps? I wondered why the majority of the first and second generation of rock/pop stars refused to let the work mature as they aged and I think it's less to do with complacency and sales than it is the strain it takes on the nervous system to continue to push the envelope. When we're young we're in fine enough shape to withstand the demands that pushing the envelope inevitably takes on the system. As we age, knowing full well we can entertain and sustain the interest of an audience without trying overly hard, the temptation might be to play the entertainer and tread water indefinitely. Priorities shift too perhaps? As George Harrison once said, many gave of themselves to help create the Beatles' success but only the four musicians gave their entire nervous systems. It's a considerable sacrifice and it takes a toll but as long as the public is with you it's arguably worth it. Once they fall away you might ask yourself, why push so hard if no one appreciates, yet alone comprehends, the effort? The answer being, you do it because you need to to stay alive. Creatively vital as opposed to economically viable (although I wish those terms weren't quite so mutually exclusive. For the fortunate few, they're not).

— **NK:** Being your own driving force, have you still found yourself, at any time, asking that question in earnest? "No one" is, perhaps, more a reflection of your inner state than of reality... .

— **DS:** Sure, I ask it of myself from time to time. It's only natural to occasionally question motivation. In fact I'd suggest it's essential that we do. When the day comes I call out and no echo returns, I'll know it's over.

— **NK:** Do you count yourself among, or at least reasonably close to, those fortunate few? I know this might have seemed like a tall order after you left Virgin, but things have changed, haven't they? You've delved into the industry yourself by creating and running samadhisound. How successful do you deem the enterprise, and what is your personal role in running it? Prior to its beginning, could you ever envision yourself as a music entrepreneur—however "organic" and small-scale?

— **DS:** No, no, not a music entrepreneur. What started out as a sort of marriage of convenience developed into something other. I'm capable of sustaining the vision needed to run a label like samadhisound but if I personally viewed it as working from within an industry as such, I'd pull the plug. This is personal, intimate, creative. There's some beautiful people that act as a buffer between me and the business end of the enterprise. Not that I don't make decisions outside of the creative aspect of running the label, I do. But I don't feel it's so different from the hand I've had in my own management over the years which has essentially been a partnership between myself and a dear friend, businessman and confidant, Richard Chadwick. But this brings me back to the notion of the periphery and my place there. We exist and, wherever possible, do business on our own terms. We've attempted to have as little to do with older models as possible looking to smaller set ups that certain robust enthusiasts have managed to sustain over a reasonably prolonged period of time. With a little research and the combined experience of all involved, we've really made things up as we've gone along.

— **NK:** Recent years spell a drastic paring down in your work; what used to be a lush garden is now buried under snow, just barely breathing. The overwhelming plenty of the cake that killed the bees is gone, replaced with the stern frugality of winter. This seems a very unlikely, if not impossible, change—even given your personal circumstances that may have contributed to it greatly. Where is the beginning of that transition, and what is, you think, its real extent? Is this a loss, a cherry orchard? A hibernation? Or a permanent shift in scale and focus, a stage completely new?

— **DS:** Nothing is permanent. Yes, a shift has taken place in life and work but it has on the whole been a revitalisation. I feel very fortunate to have found an entirely new process with which to work at this stage in my life. Well, it's been about 7 years since that shift took place with the writing and recording of "Blemish". The results and thematic content of the work are one thing but the process is independent of it although it is the means by which the work was created. A similar approach was taken when creating "Manafon". Again, the process of creating the work isn't bound to producing one kind of result. It could be applied in different settings which in turn could produce radically different results. So, that's the process. The paring down of the arrangements of recent work was necessary for the subject matter to be carried across in a suitable setting. Working with minimal means set interesting conundrums or constraints whilst at the same time offering up a certain liberty I'd not enjoyed in any other context. Thematically, on both "Blemish" and "Manafon", I wanted to address more "uncomfortable" issues. I chose not to blink. I wanted to dig a little deeper to see what surfaced. As a result they're possibly the most autobiographical of works in that they reveal myself to myself via, in part, the process of automatic writing. Okay, they may not represent the full picture but then neither does "Dead Bees" nor any of the earlier works. I chose to write about what I was experiencing which was a sort of disillusionment if you will. Sparked by a couple of major events in my life it was something I'd not experienced to quite that degree in the past so it needed to be addressed, to find out where I could go with these emotions, how to write, to find the will to write. What language was I to use? On some level it was exciting to find myself at that turning point on three fronts: process, instrumentation, thematic content. Disillusionment's just one side of the coin though. These compositions also speak of, if nothing else by the fact of their existence, the power of the creative mind. This subject is brought up repeatedly on "Manafon". It counters the sense of disillusionment as a powerful act of creative will. An affirmation of the beauty of that state of being. Will the content, the subject matter, change over time? Based on past experience I'd have to believe that's quite likely. Is it a form of hibernation? I don't believe so. Is the shift in scale permanent? I never rule anything out before conceiving a project. All doors remain open at the outset until I understand the needs of a particular work. The change was on its way long before any upsets in personal life. Prior to "Blemish" I'd been working on a number of compilations for Virgin Records as a 21 year contract came to a close. I tied up a lot of loose ends with those compilations, but it also forced me to review the work I'd produced over the previous decades. It felt as though the cycle was complete, that whatever was to come next, and I had no idea what that was to be at the time, it should be unlike what had come before. I wouldn't be returning to familiar forms in the hope of bettering myself next time round. You could reasonably argue that that had been the role of "Dead Bees". A return to familiar forms, that I loved working with, before burning down the house.

— **NK:** Burning down the house... is it possible that the need for change was so great that it couldn't be confined to work only and prompted the personal unspooling, too? In any given situation, you spend a certain amount of energy for its upkeep; what happens if you release the grip because you have to apply yourself elsewhere, because your path pulls you away?

— **DS:** A plausible scenario but not one I feel applies comfortably to my own situation.

— **NK:** How does this change compare to breaking out of Japan's cocoon?

— **DS:** It doesn't. The band was a schooling of sorts. Leaving it behind was a bit like graduating. It had been educational but had grown increasingly dysfunctional.

— **NK:** I really have to note the way you work with the notions of emotion and creative process. It's quite unusual. Emotion itself, seen as a force engulfing a human being, is habitually sanctified and glamourised as something emanating out of a higher realm— which is really, one suspects, a commonality of experience, a charmed mirror for what each of us feels at one time or another. Passive and passion: it's usually enough to be possessed by feeling, to be its subject, for that sacred glow to rub off on you. But you are obviously not content with just being a subject and letting the experience wash over you. You're an operator. "Blemish" and "Manafon" are, in a sense, surgeries you performed on yourself. Is music an instrument of survival, then? A therapy of a non-accidental kind?

— **DS:** Essentially it's an intuitive process which is always rather dull to speak of or write about as intellectually you choose to remain somewhat blind during the process of creation itself. Post mortem there's plenty that can be said but it's all so much hubris really. There's plenty of preparation or set up, there's an intuited sense where all this is leading, but until the moment comes to take action you can't foresee all of the details or intellectually know the substance of the work. But you do recognise it when it appears. Therefore, on some level, and to seemingly contradict myself, you're already on an incredibly intimate basis with the material. I don't wish to make the process sound more mysterious than it is but it lies beyond the grasp of explication, as it should. If it's a form of therapy, it's lousy at offering solutions. Cathartic? Yes, at times. Surgery is possibly an appropriate analogy for the process of internal excavation that takes place. Essentially, there's a cloud on knowing... in which you trust. There's plenty of unknowing too but over time you come to trust the direction that intuited sense of "rightness" takes you in.

— **NK:** Disillusionment: in what—or, if this is too rude a question, of what kind? You gained from the experience of creation; what did you lose before this experience became possible?

— **DS:** I lost myself.

— **NK:** You are known to excel in crafting luxurious, elaborate, polished works—beautiful but also pretty. Mellifluousness camouflaged their inner conflict so well that it could go unnoticed: at 22, I bought and sold "Weatherbox"—it sounded cold and cloying. The beauty and the sweet sorrows of it reached me years later. "Pretty" can hardly be applied to "Blemish", and even less to "Manafon". Even "Snow Borne Sorrow" offers some harsh surprises. You either refused or lost your former methods; obviously their absence became a quite unexpected presence, with very tangible things emerging out of the way you created your latest records. Your arrival to the new method—was it a choice, or has it been prompted by your inability to do things "the old way"?

— **DS:** In principle it couldn't be easier to repeat one's self, to knock out what one has done in the past but without the passion and personal investment. You don't lose it. In fact the reverse is true. You can become too tied to the forms, the themes, the comfort of familiar territory. But if the form becomes tired, exhausted, over familiar, it loses its potency to play its role effectively. The work has to NEED to be created. I continue to follow where my instincts tell me to go, which is all I'm capable of doing, whilst sustaining a totally vested interest in the outcome.

— **NK:** Is writing and playing music a part of your daily routine?

— **DS:** No, it isn't.

— **NK:** What makes you sit down and play, and how do you judge the value of the output?

— **DS:** You sit when you know something to be there... its shadow follows you around. You dabble, you dream, and slowly what was tenuous at best begins to take abstract form in your mind prior to taking absolute form.

— **NK:** With finishing "Manafon", did you feel like a gestalt was closed, a wave of emotion exhausted and worked through, or is it an open end? Is there already an inkling of what might demand to be explored next?

— **DS:** That's difficult to answer at this moment in time.

— **NK:** The armour of form came off with "Blemish". It seemed abrupt, almost demonstrative. It seemed a reaction to a large catastrophe rather than a product of evolution. But relinquishing the safety of habit in response to pain and/or change would be counterintuitive, no?

— **DS:** I have yet to work counterintuitively but I feel it's on the cards.

— **NK:** You might be close.

— **DS:** Every move I've made has been based on intuition even when deciding to work in a so called counterintuitive manner. It's not a straightforward matter.

— **NK:** Your latest work imposes the unfamiliar both on yourself and your audience, and functions similarly for both.

— **DS:** I can't claim I'm confronted with the unfamiliar. If I plan an excursion into a field of poppies I've a pretty good idea what I'm going to find there. How I use, transform, or incorporate what I find is something other.

— **NK**: With music that doesn't carry a well-defined emotional pitch (or, at least, it's too complicated to be immediately absorbed), a different kind of transmission happens—training by means of incongruity, if you will. It nurtures the ability to adjust, to get used to new and unfamiliar things rapidly. In art, eliciting emotion is most usually considered the ultimate merit, but it might not always be the biggest one.

— **DS**: Maybe the issue has something to do with our wanting, needing, recognisable signifiers, wanting to be spoon-fed? We'd like to recreate past experiences in relation to music perhaps rather than embrace new ones? Epiphanies don't have a habit of arriving on cue. They tend to reach us when the filter of expectation is removed. They come at us sideways. Occasionally art acts as a slap in the face. It challenges us to take a leap we might feel ill prepared for, but, as we've all experienced at some point in our lives, when we do finally let down our guard or resistance, marvellously dramatic changes can occur. Beauty *is*. We place parameters around what is beautiful and what's excluded from that definition. In this respect our experience of the new can be expansive, inclusive. More of the world becomes available to us in the form of nourishment, stimulation. I think we've a responsibility to attempt to create new forms, new languages, with which to speak in contemporary times. Fortunately or otherwise, they won't always feel quite as forbidding as they do to some at the outset. They will be absorbed and through absorption cultivated to the point where they too will lose their potency.

— **NK**: Have you used automatic writing before "Blemish"?

— **DS**: All writing has an element of the automatic about it if it's completed swiftly enough. The impetus for the creation of a composition comes quickly as a rule so, yes, in a sense there were years of preparation for this approach but with "Blemish" I set myself restraints that produced different results. Many elements can influence the direction a person takes in life. "Blemish" sat at the crossroads of multiple events or circumstances which had a hand in the outcome.

— **NK**: Could you describe the limitations you set for yourself?

— **DS**: Time, a limited set of means, and all the work was to be "improvised".

— **NK**: The word itself, "restraints", implies certain effort needed to remain within the boundaries... how hard was it to stay within them?

— **DS**: It was taxing applying oneself to the same restrictions on a daily basis but the results proved the restrictions effective in producing material from limited means within a strict time frame.

— **NK**: You also mentioned that restrictions liberated you: how?

— **DS**: By giving myself fewer options with which to work I applied myself to what was at hand without question, without second guessing myself. I also gave in completely to the process of automatic writing as, again, the clock was ticking and the work had to be completed with a sense of urgency and immediacy. Because of this sense of urgency (which I knew to be essential to the life of the work but wasn't sure how it'd play out in practice) I acquired a new process with which to work.

— **NK**: Would you call automatic writing and improvisation your new creative home for the time being, or are you in transit?

— **DS**: I don't feel I have a creative home. This latest process simply gives me greater options, or rather fewer limitations, as to how I approach a particular project.

— **NK**: Your new music is fearless—you're braving your own as yet unexplored abilities, the barely charted waters of improvisation, and the potential declining of your audience. But art, among other things, is limits. Fearlessness with no limits risks becoming a narcissistic rant. Discipline, structure, self-censoring—how do they fit in with automatic writing? Is there difficulty in leaving things be just as they come, rough edges and blemishes all?

— **DS:** If I'd tried this approach as a younger man the dangers would've been greater but through experience it's possible to comprehend fairly rapidly if something is working, and by working I mean it has the potential to communicate itself to others. What it is I'm pursuing is far from limitless. (The same would be true for life long improvisors. There are always some parameters in place, conscious or unconscious, self imposed or otherwise.) Although I'm coming at it by unorthodox means I know what it is I'm looking for and recognise it the moment I hear it. On the first sessions for "Manafon", held in Vienna, I gave myself 8 days to dig around and find out if this process, developed on "Blemish", could work with larger, free improvising ensembles, at play. Plenty of amazing improvisations manifested throughout those early days but I didn't find what I was looking for until the seventh day. Once I'd found it I explored that avenue for the remainder of the time I had left to me. From that point on I only gave myself one day with which to work with each successive ensemble. I knew what I was looking for and now, following on from Vienna, I knew how to get it. So much of the work is done prior to ever setting foot inside a studio via research, understanding the background, the aesthetics and flexibility of each musician involved, and selecting who should be in which ensemble with whom. These aren't random decisions made out of convenience. They're educated assessments. There are plenty of parameters in place to make sure I'm in a particular ballpark with the best fucking team I could hope to be playing with. There's plenty of discipline involved in improvisation, especially with players at the peak of their game. The dangers you feel inherent in charting this particular course could apply to most others. We're simply talking about judgment here. Judgment doesn't go out the window with improvisation. If anything it's more acute. The process of automatic writing has reached me in maturity. I've some experience with songwriting at this point in time so a lot of this is brought into play at various stages in the creation of the work. So much of it is intuitive, second nature, that I barely notice the process itself in action at the time of working.

— **NK:** Half-awake one morning, I heard music—lilting, slightly out of tune, a deaf angel choir of sorts. As soon as I did wake up, it reverted to its "reality"—commuter cars on a nearby highway. Before "Blemish", your songs were complete, insulate experiences. Now they are suggestions. Little steps towards, small nods, never entirely followed through. Catchiness is hidden, but still present. Melodies are still as much there as they were in "Dead Bees on a Cake", only in slow motion now, jointed loosely if at all. The burden of creation is shifting; so is the locus of assemblage of the emotional message. "Manafon" is practically a collaboration between yourself and our willing ears. Was this change intended?

— **DS:** There's hearing and then there's participatory listening. You have to invest in a novel, poem, painting etc. Without investment there's no real return. It's often been stated that people have to make an investment in my work. I don't feel much has changed in this respect. We're simply evolving, moving forward.

— **NK:** There is a meta-narrative formed by your personal history and your work; they form

494

a story greater than a mere sum of its parts. People follow the beautiful boy—who is yet to write "Ghosts"—into the rough terrain of "Blemish" and "Manafon". They might have turned away, failing to find a recognisable form or reference points in your latest work; but continuity of your body and name stops them from leaving. You are the experience, along with the music; in this sense, you are still a pop star. Is such thought problematic?

— **DS:** I avoid thinking along those lines but it's never been a problem for me as such. The generosity on the part of the audience has always been something I've felt immensely grateful for whatever the individual motive. For some I've moved on too far too soon perhaps but even that's to be expected in some possible scenario perhaps? At the end of my last tour in 2007, after the final night in Tokyo, physically unwell and mentally exhausted, a thought flashed through my mind with a sense of finality: "David Sylvian is dead". With that thought came an immense sense of relief. Obviously the thought was in reference to the persona, the central figure in your meta narrative. That persona, whether it was something projected unconsciously or as a means of remaining invisible, or whether it was something which was projected onto me, was now ill fitting. On that tour, midway through recording "Manafon", I began to feel the gulf between myself and the persona. I no longer inhabited it. In the world of analysis it's said that patients come to them when the personal narrative of their lives no longer holds up under current conditions. Most of the time we're able to forget or compartmentalise aspects of our lives or personality that don't fit the narrative (something I addressed on "A History of Holes", Nine Horses) but occasionally we're unable to re-write that central narrative, unable to make sense of our own lives, we unravel, come undone, lose ourselves, so we seek help. Maybe this is a problem that could be applied in the public arena too? Whatever lay behind that absurd pronouncement in my own mind, something prior, possibly fundamental, had shifted in me and being out in public had crystallised that fact.

— **NK:** Transferring "Manafon" into a live setting might be akin to taking a fish for a walk, but the "Fire in the Forest" tour did work—and beautifully—with similarly difficult material. During that tour, and in 2007, what were your reasons for taking the stage? Have you resigned to never taking "Manafon" out, or is there still uncertainty?

— **DS:** There's still a possibility, let's put it that way. I do have a specific set of requirements that would need to be in place to make the live performance work on my terms. Those specifications would be costly and involve a fair amount of creative input from others so sponsorship would be necessary. None of the previous tours undertaken were supported financially so this would be something new to me. Should there be sufficient interest in the ideas surrounding the staging of this material, I'd be unable to turn my back on it. It'd be too exciting a proposition to walk away from. Failing that, I don't see any reason at present to tour as I once did. Why tour "Blemish"? Because I wanted to see if it was possible to do so. I enjoyed the scaled down aspect of that tour and working with Takagi Masakatsu's visuals. The material was still fresh, I was still breathing the same air. The last tour of 2007 was a farewell to (the material of) the past.

— **NK:** Sharing your voice and words with people in a room can be an act of kindness, too, and quite possibly a life-changing experience for some of those present. That is, to an extent, the silver lining of "entertaining". Can it, too, be a reason for you to play live again—barring a situation where the emotional/mental price you have to pay is too great?

— **DS:** Yes, there's a beauty in that... of course... but, to be effective, it has to be more than an act of kindness. You have to embody the material, make it come alive, allow it to reinvigorate, to energise you or you won't pull it off successfully. I won't say that's never going to happen but right now it is very, very far from where I find myself.

— **NK:** Musically and personally, do you perceive yourself as a single entity moving along a timeline? Can now-David relate to the music and the mind of then-David? You often say that performing old material is a burden; are you just bored, or is the music no longer yours?

— **DS:** It's mine and it isn't mine. Is the love letter you wrote when you were thirteen yours or not? Are we the same person before and after the birth of a child, the death of a parent, surviving illness? We live many lives in one lifetime. Is it a more authentic experience to hear the Stones perform "Satisfaction" in 2010 or would it be preferable to hear it interpreted by someone younger, more fired by the emotional content of the song, feeling it for the first time? Did Jeff Buckley make Leonard Cohen's song his own? There's authorship and then there's interpretation. For my money, with the possible exception of the original recording, with the passing of time, authenticity of authorship doesn't necessarily trump the real embodiment of a song. I don't feel burdened by the material I've written but it wasn't written to fulfill any function for me past the writing and recording of the song in question. I quite unexpectedly heard "Boy With the Gun" recently and felt it stood up well. I gave each and everything all that I was able at the time. What's behind me now is out of my hands. I could perform a convincing rendition of something from "Brilliant Trees" under the right circumstances but could I do it nightly? Yes, I could, as an entertainer or interpreter of song but right now I'm not interested in playing those particular roles. Maybe that desire will return in time but as of now I want to be absorbed in new experiences that challenge me. I want to deliver something of that same quality in what I put out into the world. I don't suffer from nostalgia so I don't spend time looking back. The arc of a single life's work has merit of its own. But I wake with a sense of amnesia about the past with the exception of how something was created, how decisions were made. That's still with me.
But, generally speaking, each day is like starting from scratch.

— **NK:** The new process, obviously, brought you the excitement of the unknown. Did it bring the dizziness of danger as well? A fear of failure, perhaps: what if that path ended abruptly at a precipice? What would David do if the music left him completely? Is there anything in your life that would possibly compare to it in intensity? You make wonderful photographs that radiate both humour and melancholy—a rare, precious mix.

— **DS:** Thank you. Danger... that word again. The possibility of failure, personal and professional, is a given under most circumstances. Failure is related to a lack of concentration, vision, a lack of commitment, as much as anything else. Yes, I could fall flat on my face perhaps but is that really the worst case scenario? Can I reiterate that the creation of the work wasn't a dizzying high of some kind. I knew what I was looking for and worked out how to go about accomplishing my goals. I don't worry about music leaving me. A very odd idea. I've considered leaving it on a few occasions but only because events in my life were pulling me in other directions. If I stop making music the world keeps on turning. Yes, I may find something to replace it. That's plausible.

— **NK:** Do you feel that in place of the persona that died in Tokyo in 2007, a new one has been, or might be eventually formed? Or would you be able to live and create without defining—and letting others define—yourself anew? Is that even possible?

— **DS:** I think the recognition that the persona that was being projected was ill fitting would indicate another has taken its place. From the perspective of the onlooker changes aren't always apparent. We've made our assessments early on and we stick with them regardless of signs that indicate the portrait we've constructed no longer quite fits the subject. External perceptions are therefore slow to adjust. This happens in day to day life with people that we know, are close to. With those that we don't, that we come into contact with via media, the relationship is far more complex and an even greater reflection of ourselves.

— **NK:** "Do you know what people did in the old days when they had secrets they didn't want to share? They'd climb a mountain, find a tree, carve a hole in it, whisper the secret into the hole and cover it up with mud. That way, nobody else would ever learn the secret." You're a paradox of self-expression. The level of openness that you offer in your lyrics is astonishing. Your confessions scathe and burn. Yet you are a shy man, a self-confessed recluse thriving in almost complete withdrawal from the social milieu. How is this possible?

— **DS:** The answer is there in your question.

— **NK:** Can a poet tell a story that didn't happen to himself?

— **DS:** If the story is a means of transmission. The important elements are the philosophical and emotional authenticity that underlie the work.

— **NK:** Automatic writing must be much like dreaming—our own little theatre where we are on stage and in the audience at the same time. Does the one who is watching the play always know the plot beforehand, or is a self revealed to self as the play goes on?

— **DS:** The witness knows something but not all. Can be surprised by what is blatantly apparent to all but him/herself. Sometimes little is known at all, you learn as you go.

— **NK:** Insulated as the world of your recent collaborators might've seemed, it accepted you and rewarded your effort. It was relatively new to you; were you an element of newness to it yourself? During the improv sessions, what kind of input did you offer? As I understand it, you set out to cajole a group of artists into producing material that'd resonate with what was, at that point, your inner state, a "ding an sich". A very, very daunting task. And risky, no?

— **DS:** As I said, I wasn't certain the process itself could work until I put it into practice. I tried to reduce the element of risk as far as that was possible but a certain amount of risk was desirable. A fine balancing act in that respect. Yes, my presence changed the chemistry of the ensembles, some of whom were already very familiar with one another, in the same way that an attentive film director might bring out specifically attuned performances from the actors. They say that Bergman's face was right next to the camera lens as he directed his actors, that his focus was so nuanced and intense that the actors gave the best of themselves. He was the appreciative audience as well as director. There was an element of that at play in some of these sessions I suspect. I would like to think so.

— **NK:** Were you seeking to express an existing meaning, or was meaning formed as you went? In other words, was "Manafon" largely an aftermath of an experience or the experience itself? "Why this and not something else?": how wide was the field of potential resonance?

— **DS:** There's the experience that informs the work and then there's the work which is experience itself. There's no division as such. I suspect the field of potential resonance was drawn in the finest of lines prior to the work getting underway but there was a conscious amount of unknowing, of room for what was pre-verbal but intuited. So we'll go with "fairly narrow". This might be evidenced by the amount of material that remains unused which far outweighs what was released. The impetus for a body of work is pre-verbal, is purely intuitive, so it's fairly difficult to relay that in concrete terms to a group of free improvisers or even an individual. It was acknowledged on trust that I knew what it was I was after and the musicians involved, in all generosity, allowed me the freedom to go in search of it. I'd done my homework so it was a matter of subtly adjusting the chemical balance to react as I'd anticipated.

— **NK:** That required of you, it seems, to relinquish control — in favour of new, subtler forms of control. One of the aspects of working counterintuitively, perhaps...

— **DS:** Yes, as I said above, what is intuitive and counterintuitive isn't exactly cut and dried. True counterintuitive actions tend to be taken at the behest of others. That's where things could either come undone or become more interesting still.

— **NK:** ...and if the resonance was found, what is that sound you coaxed into being? As the environment in which the narrator moves, the music is the sound of a world that's being disassembled, functioning but just barely, a weak dissonance in place of a merry chorus, clicks and hisses where steady rhythm of machinery thumped before. It's fragile, unsafe, uncertain, it's tittering on a brink. Is this all an inner landscape, or does this reflect your feelings about the world that surrounds, contains and — to some extent — defines you?

— **DS:** It was the lack of definition, the hint, allusion, the musical and non-musical elements on the brink of dissolution. It was shorthand for the initiated, the ghost of electricity, snatches of conversation and audio intervention. It was an orchestra of the everyday. Atomic particles, the building bricks of life. Each and every sound a yantra containing a universe unto itself. It was in fact an embarrassment of riches with which to support and amplify the narrative.

— **NK:** For me, the sound evoked, and strongly, two moments of brokenness and uncertainty: when I woke up in a country without a name in 1991, and the day the towers fell in NYC. Neither of the two events affected me directly, yet they did dent my universe — and nearly everyone else's, it seems. How firmly are you rooted in the world that isn't your immediate environment? National consciousness, freedom, world peace, world suffering, wars, distant catastrophes we watch unfold on TV — what do they mean, if anything? And if they are but artificial constructs, then, perhaps, there is a better way to spend the effort invested in belonging to and fighting for them?

— **DS:** I am, of course, rooted in the world, in time and place. I've made frequent references in recent work to world events even if in a slightly unorthodox manner. Events, such as the ones you mention, burn themselves deeply into a personal and global (un)consciousness, are powerful elements of destabilisation increasing the level of uncertainty in all things. Social constructs are easily upended. The line between civility and chaos has all the substance of surface tension in a pool of water. Universal suffering is an extension of individual suffering. Universal conflict an extension of internal conflict. One cannot be resolved without the other. I believe in a society that looks after its people, a people that support one another, that lends dignity to the lives of all by seeing to basic human rights and needs, is inclusive, liberal and unafraid of difference. The greed of American capitalism was/is unsustainable. Before the value of the currency must come compassion and a shared sense of human values devoid of dogma and religious overtones. Acts of terrorism nurture the climate of fear, building walls between cultures, beliefs and individuals. They breed mistrust. By contrast natural catastrophes bring out our empathetic nature, emphasise our common humanity. You could say that, in a sense, the future depends on whether empathy or fear gains the upper hand in each of us.

— **NK:** But this precedence of internal over external is a discouraged notion these days, it seems, a Cinderella. As the culture urges to consume goods, it also urges to consume societal benefits—liberties, rights, etc., or things marketed as such. Many feel, I suspect, that those are manufactured somewhere outside of themselves, just like plastic goods at a factory in China, and can be, like any commodity, distributed by bodies of power. "None are more hopelessly enslaved than those who falsely believe they are free." (Goethe) One has to wonder how, if at all, can attention—especially in children—be directed inward as a place where meaning is formed... .

— **DS:** Children do have an interior life. In this information age they might lose sight of it a little too quickly but others withdraw into it, looking for something that might be described as self-nurturing, part of the road to independence. Whatever is absorbed from the world around us is digested internally. There is no such thing as complete objectivity. We create our own reality, are complicit in building, embracing and shouldering its responsibilities but, for all the tribal beating of drums, we're essentially alone. Don't we know this as children? I'm certain we do. A realisation that's often accompanied by sadness or fear. There's a wall between interior and exterior, illusionary perhaps, but substantial in its psychological ramifications. Via work on our interior lives the substantiality of that wall begins to evaporate hence the greater the properties of empathy and compassion in such an individual. Another's suffering becomes one's own. It takes the slightest of shifts in conscious awareness to see through the illusion and therefore to avoid buying into it. What we might grasp intuitively can find its way to the forefront of our awareness. Not to recognise your perception of reality reflected in the culture is a cause for concern that can be acted upon. Disenfranchisement, to be forced outside, can also enable a better perspective on the infrastructure of the society of all that's exclusionary about it. It's no coincidence that minority groups/outsiders appear to produce the most significant cultural contributions.

— **NK:** "Random Acts of Senseless Violence" is an especially caustic commentary on the state of "us", the society. There are (are there?) events; then (only then?) there is news. Where their meaning is formed, by whom, and to what ends, is now so obscure that it borders on arbitrary. The mechanism is called, reassuringly, "democracy". Have we spun out of control? Is the circus doomed, or is there something that each of us can do apart from registering the absurdity?

— **DS:** It would appear we're increasingly losing faith in elected officials to work with our real benefit in mind. When a nation becomes apathetic towards the governing body, when it feels its liberties being incrementally stripped away, there can only be one response beginning with protest and leading eventually to acts of disruptive violence in an attempt to be heard. Yes, the media too can't be trusted. Reporting post-9/11 more or less revealed to me there's no such thing as a free press in the US. Most reporting is framed by bias and where there's no bias there's simply a rather bland description of what is, a weak willed attempt at balanced reporting. Failing to call out and out lies as they see them but rather reporting them as another perspective on a given issue.

There's a shortage of unbiased but informed opinion. What can be done? I'm unconvinced that much can and will be done in the short term. We seem to have lost the appetite for revolution for now (although current events are changing the landscape as I write) and in a sense a revolution is needed. It would not surprise me if, increasingly, in many parts of the world, people found themselves at odds with governing bodies and their armed enforcements.

— **NK:** Is that really likely? For many, it seems, the concept of revolution, indeed the concept of any large-scale change, is a romantic one—especially without a history of violence in their own geographic realm. "Revolution" doesn't connect with the idea of ultimate upset that an actual revolution is sure to bring. "Fear of disorder" that you mention, it appears, is a safety catch, an insurance for complacency, and at its worst a complete paralysis of will: just how great the sense of danger should be to trump it?

— **DS:** It depends on what you mean by danger. A wasted life in search of the illusionary is a revelation, a dangerous revelation if reached en masse.

— **NK:** Perhaps the very bottom of the hierarchy of needs must be infringed upon for change to be able to ferment. What would your own breaking point—a transition from contempt to protest—be?

— **DS:** Possibly brazen injustice carried out or endorsed by multinational corporations or offices of governance. A corruption of the governing body to the point of arrogance, a changing of the fundamental laws which secure freedom and liberty, a watering down of democratic values. All of the above seemed within the grasp of the last US administration.

— **NK:** Truly a world citizen, you chose America as a place to stay... and thus, to act on you. Happenstance or inner affinity of a self and a place?

— **DS:** I claim happenstance but who's to decide these things?

— **NK:** Are there physical places on the planet that are of ultimate internal resonance for you?

— **DS:** There are a number of places around the globe that resonate for me but I couldn't claim that one has ultimate internal resonance. Nowhere is "home" for me... or potentially everywhere. "When you never leave your own country, you reason within your country; you become the center of the universe. When you leave, you discover there are other ways of thinking." (Charlotte Perriand) Or better still: "The man who finds his country sweet is only a raw beginner; the man for whom each country is as his own is already strong; but only the man for whom the whole world is like a foreign country is perfect." (Hugh of St. Victor 12th century)

— **NK:** "Manafon", more so than "Blemish", is a sustained narrative of disruption, entropy, alchemical nigredo, processes ongoing but misread or unsuspected. While the two records share a mood and a method, "Manafon" strives out of the insulate narrative of self and into the world at large. The world appears to to be, essentially, in the same state as the self. Is the food bitter because your tongue is bitter? Was your outlook different in happier times?

— **DS:** "Blemish" and "Manafon" don't reflect my world view. They reflect aspects of the human condition. They were born out of a time and place, a particular stimulus, a rattled state of being, yes. But that was just the starting point. I pushed deeper into those negative emotions than I would've felt comfortable doing in life. I wanted to see where they'd lead me, how dark does it get down there and what kind of language I could use on my return to embody it? The impetus for the emotional themes on "Blemish" may've been brought on by the breakdown of a marriage but I pushed far beyond the feelings I harboured in my personal life at that time. It was an opportunity to occupy a corner of my psyche I'd not previously explored. I was working with what was to hand. I was in the midst of an experience I couldn't fully digest, a lot of psychic pain, but I thought I'd face it head on without any hope of resolution. Just be with it... latch onto something powerful inside of me and hear what it had to say, how it expressed itself. We could quite easily ask this same question of filmmakers, writers etc. Bergman, Beckett, Kafka... but the works resonate because they encapsulate something of what it means to be human. A facet of our common humanity.

— **NK:** Speaking of the relationship between work and life... I may hold your music close to heart, but as I watch from afar, the David I see is only a conjecture that says more about me than about David. And that's a function of art, really, to prompt—perhaps subliminally—self-observation that often manifests itself as observation of the artist. Let's reverse the mirror: how would you describe yourself among others, what is your place in the lives of people around you?

— **DS:** In one, very real sense, as discussed, the place is peripheral, in another the role is central, pivotal. Such are the contradictions of a single life. As for the latter part of the question it's best left for others to answer.

— **NK:** How do you balance making yourself available, needing others and being needed?

— **DS:** Generally speaking, I don't manage the balance all that well. Given the choice between too much company or none at all, I'll go with the latter.

— **NK:** I can't help but notice, with certain surprise, the transactional nature of "Small Metal Gods"'s predicament. "My childish things." But you're throwing them away just as childishly: they didn't serve the purpose, you've been defrauded out of your money in the marketplace of faith, where peace and well-being are given in return for worship... I suspect that this obvious reading is wrong.

— **DS:** The lyric is slightly bitter, quite petulant, disillusioned, angry. It's not in the least bit rational. There's a tit for tat aspect to it on one level but it's also about superstition, false gods, the adopted traditions of others. It's a "let's see what's real" moment. Let's sweep these trinkets away (physical objects yes, but all that they represent as emotional and spiritual investment) and see what's left standing. A cleaning house. It happens every so often. I don't find it unhealthy. It's a search for truth by removing the excess baggage that's begun to cling to it like lint to a black overcoat. But the anger shouldn't be underestimated. I heard from a number of people that have followed one path or another, that they felt a sense of release/relief hearing that lyric. As if permission had to be granted to call all into question. It had to have that degree of the irrational, the petulance, to get across the degree of personal investment, anger and disillusionment. Not dissimilar to the kind of conversations you hear between divorcing couples.

— **NK:** In relation to the practices of faith that you maintain, who are they, the castaway gods? Is it an intentional "sacrilege", questioning elements of the path while still remaining on the path? Jettisoning the paraphernalia that had served its purpose, but now might prove a hindrance?

— **DS:** Even when you reject the path, refuse to believe in the path, you're on the path.

— **NK:** One way or another, "Small Metal Gods" seems to rid you of the last outward vestiges of the very path you adhere to. Where is this going?

— **DS:** Where is this going? Where it was always going. It's referred to as a path but it's anything but linear. Sometimes to take action, any action, is better than none at all.

— **NK:** Imagery of devotion is often found in your writings—from various sources, as if you were sampling, trying on this faith and that. You say much—any?—of it doesn't hold any significance. When you chose your current path, what revealed it to you as yours? Was it a gradual immersion, or was there a moment of "marriage"?

— **DS:** Difficult to answer this one as it's too personal. I would say that to experience states of bliss is to acknowledge the existence of alternate states of mind, of being. If an individual brought you to that state there's a fair chance, but by no means a certainty, that they'll make a good scout leading you into uncharted territory.

— **NK:** I'll play a devil's advocate a little—without implying your case, but with interest in your take on the following. One ends up subscribing to a set of exercises, to a certain philosophy, to a picture of the world—even if that picture is one of freedom to change it at will. But the practices of any spiritual tradition, before having been assigned "sacredness", were designed for a specific time, place, and people, and with specific outcomes in mind; hence outside its "native" circumstance its techniques might be useless, if not downright harmful. These traditions are still perfectly capable of instilling a sense of emotional wellbeing in their followers, but no real growth transpires. This doesn't mean the practices are inherently empty; there is, let's say, a great chance for them to be misapplied. Perhaps a teacher, a presence which can observe and reflect your condition objectively, can be a remedy, a true beacon for your travels. At any given time, how do you judge your position on the way? Is there someone to help you with this?

— **DS:** I wouldn't agree that all spiritual practices derived from profound insight and wisdom were designed for a time and place. What was once a fundamental or universal truth about human nature likely remains so but it's not my place to take a defensive position on this. If interested, we should work this through for ourselves. Judging where one is on any given path is difficult. I'm not at all certain that that's an appropriate question to pose oneself. It's stating that you believe you're at point Q on the map on the road to Z. Linear thinking. The way it works is to let go of such mental concepts whilst recognising a deepening of certain qualities within, and the greater awareness that accompanies these developments. You therefore recognise the benefit of cultivating this particular conscious awareness. That's where you are, just there.

— **NK:** What does following a path mean to you? Obviously, many teachings are being relentlessly appropriated by western mind and market for their own purposes. Most often they end up functioning as pacifiers, numbing hearts to the very notion of path as work. Placated, the "adepts" tend to neglect and isolate exactly the parts of themselves that require change, control and attention. The product sells and is, infuriatingly, called "spirituality". But the stories of spiritual development that so many choose to ignore speak of anything but comfort. Choosing a path, wedding yourself to it might be the greatest joy you ever knew; what about following it? Were there obstacles, and was music ever one, in any way?

— **DS:** I don't feel comfortable saying I'm wedded to a particular path. I say that with a certain regret as I believe one travels more rapidly when adhering to a singular path. As for teachings being appropriated, sure. If you want to divest yoga of its spiritual "baggage" you're free to do that. If you choose to meditate just to relax, that's okay too. I don't think it's productive to worry about what others are doing or how they're using, diluting, or abusing the teachings. What is of concern is how they're applied, if at all, in one's own life, how sharply attuned is one's own sense of discernment? After all, one man could sit at the feet of the wisest of individuals and learn nothing, another at the feet of a faker and take away valuable lessons.

— **NK:** Duly noted... an accusatory diatribe indeed most often reflects one's own stumbling blocks — and, in this particular case, locks one out of a potentially beneficial experience. You say there isn't a singular path; this, perhaps, is not a cause for regret, since there is no real way to assess its comparative effectiveness. You're on the best path possible — for you — winding as it might be. What is your current set of practices — or, at least, a system (systems?) of reference? How rigorously do you follow it?

— **DS:** This I choose to remain private.

— **NK:** Earlier, the terminology of certain teachings was figuring prominently in your songs — "The Golden Way", "Cover Me with Flowers", etc. With time, it was gone almost completely. How would you describe the process that reflected in this change?

— **DS:** From the romance of the engagement (which is real and healthy) to the reality of the contract (the vow), to a disentanglement from all that binds.

— **NK:** Is there a destination? What would you want to become, ideally — or at least approach? Is being compassionate, responsible, loving the purpose or a satellite effect of a larger change?

— **DS:** When following a path surely the only real concern is with your personal growth and what furthers that? (As this tends to result in a more compassionate, responsible, and loving individual we all benefit.) Yes, there are always obstacles, each one greater than the last but there are rewards for scaling these, otherwise there wouldn't be the will to go on as suffering is pretty much a given. As with any undertaking there should be discernible results. Knowing the scope for self deception is vast, you tread carefully but purposefully. Being long-term goal oriented doesn't seem quite the point. Maybe this contradicts the notion that there should be discernable results but how can you comprehend a destination for this approach to life at the outset? Goals should therefore be manageable, humble, not overly ambitious. Sitting on a cushion for 15 minutes morning and evening without giving in to the desire to reach for the iPhone? In essence you're already where it is you want to be. Think of it as a dream you're having, part joyful, part nightmare, in which you're trying to get back to the safety, the familiarity of your bedroom. You wake up where you were all along. "You misunderstood the place where you stand." Long term, so as not to cop out of giving some indication; call it... call it an attunement to where the division between life and death falls away. Not an end in itself. Yes, making music has been part of the process for me.

— **NK:** Could you expand on this?

— **DS:** The process of creating music is fraught with dilemmas that highlight shortcomings, entrenched thought processes, self-imposed limitations etc. It has the potential to identify and therefore remove obstacles to growth. It's what is known as "sadhana": Sadhana Sanskrit term: literally "a means of accomplishing something".

— **NK:** Lyrics and poetry. To you, what is the difference? "Manafon"'s words stand on their own, it seems, much more ably than those of your other records. They are certainly not orphaned without music; there is no obvious dependency. But in the way they came into being, how strong was the connection?

— **DS:** The lyrical content was generally born out of my response to the musical content although there were themes I knew I'd be addressing in some instances before putting pen to paper. They're also, in my mind, tied to the melodic lines that define them as they were more or less created simultaneously.

— **NK:** This works both ways, doesn't it? The language in action, a word being uttered, is in itself music, and much music is—often unconsciously—modelled on the inflections of speech and other expressive sounds. The two meanings—verbal and tonal—converge or collide, often to a striking effect. You've been using this method, knowingly or not, with great success throughout your career... .

— **DS:** It's part and parcel of the songwriting experience, yes. I've said before that the difference between a lyric and a poem is that between the lines of a lyric there's silence which is where the music plays its significant role. The writing is designed for this purpose. Between the lines of a poem, a universe. Any addition is embellishment.

— **NK:** Your singing has also undergone a transformation. What is your relationship with your voice? How did it change over the years?

— **DS:** I find it impossible to discuss my voice. Possibly detrimental, certainly undesirable.

— **NK:** "Manafon" is cutting; it's words of a man who is either done for and is about to flip a switch, or has purposely dismantled his reality. Were you trying to sing yourself out of that mindset, is the audible pain a productive suffering, a black and bitter but fertile soil? Or is "not leaving a trace" an earnest goal?

— **DS:** I thought it was an album best released posthumously.

— **NK:** Your writing is exceptionally erudite; quotes and references abound—from Picasso to Sartre, from the Bible to R. S. Thomas and—heartbreakingly—Emily Dickinson... . Are they simply magnets to you, something that resonated with you at the moment of writing, or do the nods signal an allegiance, a very special connection? Are there figures, teachings, works of art that are beyond reproach, or is everything malleable?

— **DS:** I think my approach in this regard has changed over the years. When younger the isolated man wanted a creative community with which to interact. I formed allegiances with artists both living and dead whose vision I grasped, in which I saw reflected something of my own feeble attempts though expressed far more eloquently. A shared philosophical viewpoint, aesthetic etc. etc. I phased out much of the openly quoted from my work during the late '80s, early '90s. Now if someone is quoted it's because the quote clearly serves a purpose, other than simple reference, in the body of the lyric.

— **NK:** Do you have "fathers"? Would you say that musically, intellectually, and emotionally you had influences that made you what you are? Did any of those hinder your movement once you've gone past the stage of absorption? Was reverence ever a stumbling block?

— **DS:** When younger reverence might've been a slight stumbling block, I can't be certain. In that I couldn't always bring myself to say no to invitations by those I respected. I believe there's always something to be learned through experience of any kind so nothing in a sense is lost but time. I do believe there were periods where I should've remained silent. It would be a blessing if an artist could erase his failures or under achievers and leave only that which served a purpose on his/her departure. It might drive biographers and archivists up the wall but the world would be a better place for the absence of such works. This isn't said from a position of vanity merely the recognition that there's too much to avail yourself of in a single lifetime. Best not waste time searching in the wrong quarter for what lies elsewhere.

— **NK:** You work alone. Once you're done with the contributions, the process becomes invisible. Is this a comfort or a necessity?

— **DS:** Both.

— **NK:** You once said, "Periphery, in every aspect of life, is my rightful place." It's easy to read withdrawal into it, a policy of not taking part, but you, I suspect, meant something different.

— **DS:** I feel I am taking part in some cultural exchange however humble my contribution. The periphery is where I find myself. I fought the inevitable for a fairly long time and then... I didn't. I embraced it. Many lessons in life are resolved by embracing what is.

— **NK:** For what transpires with and within yourself, are you an onlooker? A chronicler rather than a sword-wielding knight? If so, do you feel that the writing process you now employ is, perhaps, a better fit for this position—and thus a logical development?

— **DS:** I think, ideally, one is witness and participant.

— **NK:** Speaking of taking part... having children is obviously as drastic a case of involvement as can be. An immense joy, but also an ocean of thin ice to cross. What is the journey like for you? How did it change you?

— **DS:** Oh dear, that's an entirely independent subject of conversation. To state the obvious, it changes one's priorities. A disarmingly short sentence that denotes major shifts in one's outlook on life. It introduces you to unconditional love and, on the path of non-attachment, presents you with all you'll ever need to work with.

— **NK:** For those of us for whom it's still ahead... what proved to be the most (and perhaps unexpectedly?) rewarding in being a father?

— **DS:** Beckett could've written his oft quoted line; "Fail again, fail better" for parents because our shortcomings are underlined every single day of our lives. But the beauty is that the love remains constant. "Forgiveness" is another of those words bandied about a great deal but to feel it in your heart towards another, or to feel it directed towards oneself (by a child?) [is] quite powerful stuff. If we practiced forgiveness and gratitude every day of our lives we'd be transformed.

— **NK:** Some say birth is a clean slate, but where the real beginning is, we can't know. When you first knew yourself from everything else, what did you see? What kind of world did you inhabit as a child?

— **DS:** I don't believe birth to be a clean slate. From what I've experienced we come into the world (most of us/all of us?) with quite a bit of baggage or unfinished business. It's difficult to recall a time when I wasn't alienated by my surroundings. There was an awareness of the sense of separation, myself and the other, and the desire to be part of the world I could see around me but they appeared to be mutually exclusive. I'm uncertain how reliable such recollections are but I think this was a sensation I struggled with when young. I wanted to be absorbed into the body of the mother, the family, not excluded (the exclusion was only in the form of the awareness of my independence). I inhabited the world of my imagination for the most part. Steve and I were always very close. Distinctly different from one another in so many respects, but close. Like most kids, we invented games and scenarios and acted them out. My parents were never financially secure so we weren't inundated with gifts, toys, even the pleasure of their company was rationed as they always seemed to have so much on their plates, so we were left to our own devices.

— **NK:** You grew up and spun away, far away from your nest—so far that to an outside observer it might seem like you never belonged there at all. Did you ever go back, with a new understanding? Are you in touch with your parents?

— DS: No, I never returned. It's fair to say I didn't feel as though I belonged. Yes, I'm in touch, and have a beautiful relationship with my parents.

— NK: What sustains you these days? It's very easy to focus on the melancholy in your work: you have, after all, expressed it so powerfully; we seek comfort in sharing these emotions, and they're part of a compelling human drama. But you are still pressing on, and that is where things get even more interesting. As the world loses all colour and distinction, how do you keep on keeping on?

— DS: We're able to survive on very little it seems to me. Simple human kindness perhaps? Melancholy is a word I've never liked, never use. It doesn't burn deeply enough. "There's comfort in melancholy" Joni Mitchell once sang. I've been where that comfort doesn't exist.

— NK: But melancholy, as opposed to acute pain, is a part of a natural disposition of a witness, no? And itself a kind of a force...

— DS: We see things differently I guess. Melancholy appears somewhat impotent to me. A safety blanket for the soul. We frequently reach for it perhaps but maybe we should learn to live without it?

— NK: I feel this disagreement lies in the realm of words, not thoughts. Maybe we should learn to live without behaving like a textbook (passive?) "melancholic", and instead face the sadness of the world with love, acceptance and resolve, like brave tin soldiers.

— DS: When my daughter comes to me in tears and says she feels sad for no reason, after questioning her to make sure nothing is untoward, I tend to tell her this is part of what it is to be human and to enjoy the easy, freefalling tears, experience how good it feels to express herself (she breaks into laughter when I say this as it's never what she expects to hear). God knows in later life sadness isn't expressed so purely and beautifully. ... Has the world lost all its colour? Some, perhaps. But the cover of "Manafon" depicts a visual metaphor for the dwelling place of the imagination. It's abundant.

— NK: Can the realms of imagination and everyday life be one?

— DS: Well, what is imagination and what is everyday life? Who/what imagines that everydayness?

— NK: Do you expect the colours to return someday, the damage to be repaired—or at least lose some of its importance?

— DS: I do, and then some.

— NK: There is no undoing it, obviously, no erasing the scars, but there is light ahead, isn't there?

— DS: There's light everywhere. Even when the soul is in darkness the witness knows this to be true. It's a source of strength, enables endurance. Is death and its shadow presence or absence? Everywhere you turn there's beauty and sorrow. It's overwhelming. It is my work, it does represent me but somehow I shouldn't be entirely confused with what it is I produce.

— NK: You are not. Shadow of death is definitely a quickening presence, though no bugbear... . What is death to you?

— DS: Transition.

— NK: In this culture that, heartbreakingly, deems aging a catastrophe and sells afterlife for good behaviour, how does it feel to have reached a late middle age?

— **DS**: Because of my mental make-up I've always welcomed aging. With the sheen of youthful beauty and the radiance of innocence gone something other takes its place. Age has a beauty all its own that is suitably timely. There's a liberation of sorts from the superfluous, the surface of things: "You looked into mirrors/where death was at work/of that you were certain/but it was all surface/and surface is numb". It's time to work.

— **NK**: Tell us about the rabbits. Hunted in "Brilliant Trees", killed and skinned in "Manafon". Are you casting yourself on both sides of the hunt?

— **DS**: The hunting metaphor in relation to the act of creation has a long lineage. Also in relation to the persecution of artists disapproved of by the state. The scapegoat.

— **NK**: "And if everything still matters, what then?"—"There is no maker, just inexhaustible indifference." And here, to an outside ear, you sound quietly exhilarated. Do you consider the question answered?

— **DS**: I fail to differentiate between the emptiness and the fullness. Whatever the outcome "I" as artifact, false construct, illusion, will not go on. Yes, there's comfort in that.

— **NK**: Everyone has a horizon, that line we can't see past—not in ourselves, and not in others. The hope of reaching it dies hard, it seems, so we keep running. Are you still running?

— **DS**: I've never considered this horizon. I can't seem to locate it. I've experienced bound-lessness, infinite love and peace. I've also known the distress and claustrophobia of being absented from that. If running, it's usually away from self, away from, or towards death. There are many kinds of death in life. If you're not ready for the one you have to face there will be struggle, yes, running. If I'm running I took the precaution of taking my vows to the pursuit of "truth" so I can't get far. Witness and participant.

07/14 - MANAFON

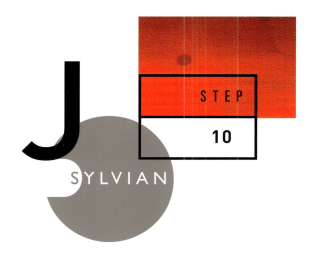

J

SYLVIAN

STEP

10

MANAFON

SMALL METAL GODS

It's the farthest place I've ever been
It's a new frontier for me
And you balance things
Like you wouldn't believe
When you should just let things be

Yes, you juggle things
'Cause you can't lose sight
Of the wretched storyline
It's the narrative that must go on
Until the end of time

And you're guilty of some self neglect
And the mind unravels for days
I've told you once
Yes, a thousand times
I'm better off this way
I'm better off this way

Where's my Queen of Hearts
My royal flush
I've cleaned and scrubbed her decks
My suicide, my better days
There's nothing I regret

I've placed the gods
In a ziploc bag
I've put them in a drawer
They've refused my prayers
For the umpteenth time
So I'm evening up the score

Small metal gods
From a casting line
From a factory in Mumbai
Some manual labourer's bread and butter
And a single-minded lie

Small metal gods
Cheap souvenirs
You've abandoned me for sure
I'm dumping you, my childish things
I'm evening up the score.

THE RABBIT SKINNER

Who'll do for him
Child of the '50s
With no common sense
And no easy resting place
Only lichen on beeches
Oil on gun barrel
And the hard taste of pennies

A gardener's folly
Stands as proud as you please
The lungs won't fill, the heart won't start
Landlocked child of the seas
And he alone is a man without qualities

Combed his body for disorders
But the disease lived on in far off quarters

As a God everything was filled to excess
As a man he settled for less

Here lies the rabbit skinner
God love the rabbit skinner

A life without purchase
No story to tell
And three little bitches fight where he fell.

Foxes, foxes, give her a sign
Enter the little girl and show her what's mine

Play hard and fast with the rules if you please
Here lies a man without qualities

RANDOM ACTS OF SENSELESS VIOLENCE

Under yellow light
Comes the face of tomorrow
Lights the fuse gives meaning to
All that was previously hollow

To a soundtrack of sirens
And mute aspiration
The express train to Heathrow
First of the morning
Is leaving the station

Our reckless sun rises
On the tip of the iceberg
Hidden in plain sight
Still alive and full of surprises
A generation gone soft
Over new acquisitions
That can't take the edge off

I've put away my childish things
Abandoned my silence too
For the future will contain
Random acts of senseless violence

The targets hit will be non-specific
We'll roll the numbers, play with chance
All suitable locations
Unplanned in advance

Someone's back kitchen
Stacked like a factory
With improvised devices
There's bound to be injuries
With improvised devices
No phone-ins, no courtesy
No kindness

And the future will contain
Random acts of senseless violence

And it's not just the boredom
It's something endemic
It's the fear of disorder
Stretched to its limits
And the safety in numbers is just a contrivance
For the future will contain
Random acts of senseless violence

Democracy is very
Democracy is very merry

THE GREATEST LIVING ENGLISHMAN

Here we are then, here we are
Notes from a suicide
And he will never ever be
The greatest living Englishman

It's such a melancholy blue
Or a grey of no significance
Plastic coated surfaces
A space to place his suitcase
As he's bussed from A to B

But it's such a melancholy blue
The curtains 'round the bed are drawn
Broadcast voices from the ward
The humming of machines are heard
But there are distances between
Yes, there are distances between

His aspirations visited him nightly
And amounted to so little
Too much self in his writing
Now he will never ever be
The greatest living Englishman

The engine shifts into second gear
They're all aboard accounted for
It's a journey he must make alone
The black sheep boy is leaving home

It's been rehearsed a thousand times
or more
He's well prepared of that he's sure

But still it's such a melancholy blue
He's erased a page of history
Much as he'd intended to

He wouldn't speak or show you he was happy
Though you'd meet him with your eyes
There was a wall that always stood between you
He'd shut himself outside

And the love that he engendered
Would never be enough
For him to feel alive
Warm and tender
He'd shut himself outside

Not a fake nor a sham
But dug in deep and fighting
The world could not embrace a man
With so much self in his writing

And he was never gonna be
The greatest living Englishman
He had ideas above his station
Minor virtues go unmentioned

Little England you fit like a straightjacket
Hemmed by the genius of others
He said "to conquer the
world is not to leave a trace
remove even the shadow of the
memory of your face"

A grey of no significance

125 SPHERES

And when it appeared
It was a flaming book of matches
A hundred and twenty-five spheres
On a parquet floor

SNOW WHITE IN APPALACHIA

Half-life
She moves in a half-life
Imperfect

She'd abandoned them there
In the hills of Appalachia
She threw off the sandbags
To lighten the load

From her place on the stairs
Or sat in the backseat
Sometimes you're only a passenger
In the time of your life

As soon as the sun rose
The keys were in the ignition
Following the tyre tracks
Of the truck sanding the road

And there's snow on the mattress
Blown in from the doorway
It would take pack mules and provisions
To get out alive

There had to be drugs
Running through the girl's body
There had to be drugs
And they too had a name

There were concerts and car crashes
There were kids she'd attended
And discreet indiscretions
For which she'd once made amends

And the adrenalin rush
Had left her exhausted
When under the blue sky
Nothing need be explained

And there's ice on the windshield
And the wipers are wasted
And the metal is flying
Between her and her friends

And there is no maker
Just inexhaustible ndifference
And there's comfort in that
So you feel unafraid

And the radio falls silent
But for short bursts of static
And she sleeps in a house
That once too had a name

EMILY DICKINSON

She was no longer a user
Don't think she realised we knew that
Not one to make a fuss
Why this and not something else
Wasn't it obvious?

She made such a hash of it
You can't help but notice
A near absence of tenderness
And who wants to live like that?

And friends turned their backs on her
She, no longer a user
And she wanted to stay home
With a box full of postcards
And no place to send them
Live like Emily Dickinson
Without so much as a kiss
Or the comfort of strangers
Withdrawing into herself
But why this and not something else?

Dead Letters

THE DEPARTMENT OF

MANAFON

There's a man down in the valley
Who doesn't speak in his own tongue
He bears a grudge against the English
The tune to which his songs are sung

There's a man down in the valley
Who is moving back in time
It's a physical ascension
You can watch him as he climbs

The farmer's wives are at their windows
They've seen him wind his way for hours
They tell the kids to lower their voices
And pretend that they are out

There's a man down in the valley
Trying to stop time in its tracks
His boots lie heavy on the grasses
But it keeps on pushing back

And his wife she was a painter
But now she stains the altar black
He's out bird watching on the islands
And she wishes he'd come back

There's a man down in the valley
And he dreams of moving west
Of battles raged against the furies
That might see him at his best

There's a man down in the valley
Don't know his right foot from his left

Don't know his right foot from his left

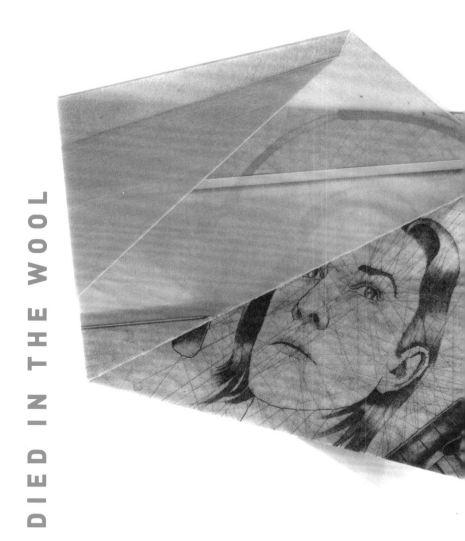

DIED IN THE WOOL

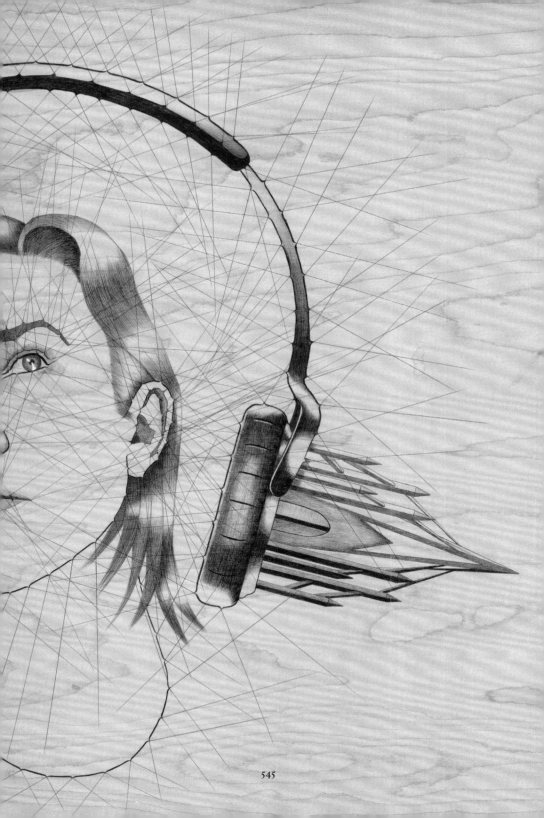

FIVE LINES (THE CRY OF THE ORNITHOLOGIST)

Five lines
Five lines with which he marked time
Five lines flared from the ovens

He pulled the ribbons from their hair
With melodies beaten from the sheets of his mother
Songs for the end of time

Five lines returned the birds to their singing

The sun fell
(Should we leave it to the foxes)
The sun fell from the sky
(Leave it to its wits and its devices)
The sun fell from the sky in the form of a stag
Buried deep in the forest

And that's where he found it
A blow to the head had left it unconscious
Nothing further was said

We'll set a place for him
We'll set a place then

For he had tried
Blood-bone-feathers to the sky
But even in flight
Nothing could've spared him

Five lines
Five lines flared from the ovens
Five lines with which he marked out time

Leave him for the foxes

DIED IN THE WOOL

Is this how they'll find her?
Pale blue frock coat
Snagged full of needles
Belly full of sunshine?

And what will they do without him
Now she's gone?
What will they do without him?

The sheep on the hill alert in the darkness
The ears of the darkness startled by thunder
Gathered for safety
They dressed her in wool coats

And what will they do without him
Now she's gone?

What will they do?

The hair that was blonde is matted and brown
The heft of her body impresses the ground
Softened by rainfall soaked right through
The lightening sky and the darkening blue

And what will they do now she's gone?

Give her your shoes boy, lend her some threads
A fine line of linen stripped from your bed
What's with the face child?

The smaller the bird the closer it stood
Coming still closer from the edge of the woods
In the down of the den six hearts lie beating

The ground softens up and welcomes her in
You've been gone so long honey
Where have you been?
You were destined for better
Surely nothing so cruel
What once was unwritten's
Died in the wool

The hair that was blonde is matted and brown
The weight of her body impresses the ground
Softened by rainfall soaked right through
The lightening sky and the darkening blue

Is this how they'll find her
Last ounce of courage
Face full of sunshine?

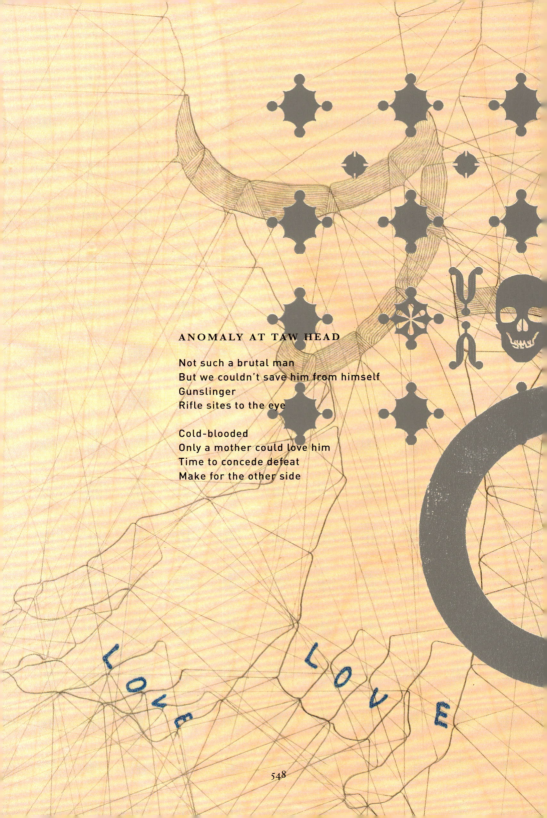

ANOMALY AT TAW HEAD

Not such a brutal man
But we couldn't save him from himself
Gunslinger
Rifle sites to the eye

Cold-blooded
Only a mother could love him
Time to concede defeat
Make for the other side

THE LAST DAYS OF DECEMBER

What shall we tell them
A honeymoon brief as a walk in the park?
What shall we tell them when they ask
And they'll ask
Could you not see another way out?

Was the place without sun, was it furnished in black
With the ache of the gas oven there at your back?
A death angel paces in boredom and waits
It shrieks from dark corners undermining your faith

What shall we tell them when they ask
And they will ask
Could you not see another way out?

Where were the cape and the coastline
The wonder kid's sunshine?

Your sanity shattered and climbing the walls
Wet towels at the floor line stuffed under the doors
And the beating of powder-black wings left you blind
The last days of December are the loneliest kind

In the exit you made there was no pause for thought
'Cause the lies that I told were the lies that you bought
There was no place to find you no you to be found
In the margins of books you were reading
There are stages to grieving that won't let you down

Where was the coastline, the wonder kid sunshine?

Under northern skies anonymous and free
Your night fisherman pushes a boat out to sea
He'll surely meet yours though his faith is unsound
There are stages to grieving that won't let you down.

NEITHER LITANY NOR LAMENT

FROM THE OUTSET YOU WERE DISRUPTIVE
CLASS CLOWN LOUD, CLAMOURING FOR ATTENTION
ROTUND, HEAVIER THAN I'D BE EVEN IN ADULT LIFE
YOUR INCLINATION TO RIDICULE FOR LAUGHS
THE WEAKNESSES OF SELF AND OTHERS BEFORE THE CLASS
BETRAYED A VULNERABLE HEART
ME, TOO SELF-CONSCIOUS TO WILLINGLY DRAW FIRE
KEPT SAFE A DISTANCE
YET NO ONE IT APPEARED WILLINGLY ASPIRED
TO SIT AT YOUR SIDE
WHAT MIGHT BE ADDED THAT OPPOSITES ATTRACT?
EXHIBITIONIST SEEKS OUT THE UNCOMMONLY SHY
BOYS! MULTIPLY X TO THE POWER OF Y

ON LUNCH BREAK WINDING OUR WAY BACK FROM THE SHOPS
WE BROKE OFF FROM THE OTHERS
FELL BACK IN DISCOMFORTING SILENCE
NEITHER ONE AS YET SURE OF OUR FOOTING
I ASKED WERE YOU HAPPY AS YOUR BEHAVIOR IMPLIED
YOUR FACE, SUSPICIOUS OF TRUST
SENT BACK ECHOES FROM A DARKER PLACE

OPENLY DISLOYAL YOU WERE TO BECOME OBSESSED
POSSESSED BY THE CORNERSTONE OF YOUR UNDOING
YOU TORTURED HIS YOUNG MIND WITH VICE-LIKE INTENSITY
THE TIGHTENING WHITE BONE OF YOUR SKULL PRESSED IN ON YOUR OWN
A BRUISING WASTELAND OF DARK WINTER NIGHTS
PHONE CORD OF A NERVOUS SYSTEM WOUND TIGHT
UMBILICAL DELIVERY OF PUNISHING CALLS
YOUTH PERCHED ON THE LOWER STAIRS OUT IN THE HALL
AN ADULT EDUCATION, A GROOMING IN LOYALTY
LONG BEFORE YOURS MET THE RIGHT HAND OF ROYALTY

A CHEMICAL DISRUPTION, THE SPAWN OF A VIRUS
THAT SEEMED DESTINED TO DISABLE THE ARC OF A LIFE
DISSATISFIED, SULLENLY REPENTANT
MOUTH AROUND HIS COCK YOU SUCKED AND SUCKED
MADE HIM IMMUNE TO LOVE

IMAGINARY WOUNDS, WRONGS AND OFFENCES
PERPETRATED BY HIM RATTLED YOU SENSELESS
"YOU THINK HE'S GOOD BUT YOU DON'T SEE WHAT I SEE"
AND WE COULDN'T
THERE WAS NOTHING BUT A COWED CHASTENING
A DOGGED LOYALTY TO A NEAR FATAL STRAND OF NARCISSISM

THE WEIGHT WAS LOST AND IN ITS PLACE
A BRITTLE MAN OF BONE SPLINTERING FEROCITY
NURSING A KELOID COVERED HEART
I TOO BECAME THE FOCUS OF A MAGNIFICENT FURY
A VIOLENT RESENTMENT THAT SAT JUST BENEATH THE THIN SKIN
OF YOUR UPROARIOUS GOOD HUMOUR
IMAGINED ENEMY, COMPETITOR AGAINST WHOM YOU'D CONSPIRE
HUMILIATION AND A CHANGE OF ALLEGIANCES
THE ANTICIPATED PAYOFF
IT NEVER OCCURRED TO YOU TO AIM HIGHER

BUT YOU COULDN'T HELP YOURSELF
OR SO WE THOUGHT
AND WHEN ON FORM YOU CHARMED LIKE NO OTHER
A STONED-HEADED SELF-DEPRECATING WELLSPRING OF LAUGHTER

LAST WE MET DECADES AGO
A LONG DEMOLISHED ESTABLISHMENT ON THE KING'S ROAD
WALKING ON EGGSHELLS WITH AGGRESSIVE TIMIDITY

SHOULD ONE FALSE MOVE TIP THE SCALES OF CIVILITY
YOU INVITED ME BACK INTO YOUR LIFE
FLATTERINGLY CLAIMING I BROUGHT OUT THE BEST
BUT ONE WEEK LATER I WAS AGAIN CUT OFF
CAST OUT WITH THE REST
WHAT IMAGINED WRONG HAD BEEN SUSTAINED IN THE INTERVAL?
WHAT SMALL GIFT HAD BEEN HANDED AS JUSTIFICATION?
YOU'D CHOSEN A SIDE, ONE YOU'D REPEATEDLY TAKEN OUR ENTIRE LIVES
AND IN TAKING SIDES THE INDEPENDENCE THAT WAS
RIGHTFULLY OURS WAS SURRENDERED
YOUR TRUTH A LIE
ESPOUSED FROM TWIN MASKS OF OUTRAGE AND VICTIMISATION
NO EXPLANATION, NO QUARTER GIVEN
NONE TAKEN

THE HURT AND CONDEMNATION
PERMANENTLY FORMED ON YOUR LIPS
THE MIND GREW VIOLENT
YOU BROADCAST VANITY
ASSURED OF MY SILENCE

THE COMPASS OF YOUR MIND KNEW NO REST
SWINGING NORTH TO SOUTH, SOUTH EAST TO WEST
A MAGNETIC TOY FOR UNKNOWN FORCES
OF A POWERFULLY MALEVOLENT ANCIENT ORDER THAN MOST HAVE TO SHOULDER

SO, MAY THE COMPASS COME TO REST
ON THE STILL POINT OF ETERNITY
MAY YOUR DEMONS DISSOLVE IN THE
BUFFOONISH CHARITY OF YOUR LAUGHTER
WHAT WAS LONGED FOR WAS THERE IN THE MAKING
YOU'VE DONE ENOUGH, TIME FOR GRATITUDE
IT'S THERE FOR THE TAKING

IMPLAUSIBLE BEAUTY

SO YOU FIND YOURSELF
SUMMONED TO IT
YOU WISH THERE'D BEEN A DIFFERENT PATH
ONE NOT QUITE SO PUBLIC
HUMILIATION ACCOMPANIES YOU TO BED EACH NIGHT
THE BURNING RED OF IT
WHY CONFESS, WHY OWN UP TO WHAT YOU SPEND YOUR DAILY LIFE
TRYING TO CONCEAL?
YOU'D INTENDED TO CHANGE YOUR NAME
JETTISON THE SANDBAGS OF YOUR OWN PAST THAT YOU MIGHT RISE
LIGHTER INTO THE MOMENT, UNENCUMBERED
IN THE NOW OF NO ONE
YOU'D IMAGINED A SMALL ISLAND
WITH SOLITARY BEACH
SOLITARY IN THAT IT WAS FOR YOU ALONE
YOU AND THAT LOVED ONE
THE ONE YOU'VE BECOME TOO DESPERATE TO POSSESS
BECAUSE THE SMELL OF DESOLATION IS UPON YOU
YOUR NEED TOO GREAT
THEY SCATTER LIKE MICE TO THE WALLS WHEN YOU ENTER
AND YET HERE YOU ARE BENEATH THE LIGHTS
LISTENING TO YOUR VOICE RESOUND AROUND THE ARCHITECTURE
PLACES YOU'D OTHERWISE NEVER FREQUENT
LOVER OF SOLITUDE IN SO MANY WAYS IN NEED OF ANOTHER
TONIGHT YOU'LL DO THEIR BIDDING
BECAUSE THEIR NEED IS ABSOLUTE
AND THIS BEING THE CASE, WHERE ELSE WOULD YOU RATHER BE?

WRITING HOME

If there's the murdering kind
That there's a provocative mind
And I'll kill every surgeon that dares bring it water
This here's the pummeling fist
Your stars at birth promised you this
It bloodies the mouth that's calling for order

And it was always this way
Raw like a circle of lions
Don't overextend your stay
Dear father
The exit was part of the plan
The house is riddled with wires
I'm taking you home by the hand
Dear father

Outside the wrestling ring
The local church choirboy sings
Laments for the violent times of others
The wards are taken in shifts
The dead press a kiss to your lips
The sisters want back the beds for their mothers

And it was always this way
Raw like a circle of lions
Don't overextend your stay
Dear father
The exit was part of the plan
This house is riddled with wires
I'm taking you home by the hand
Dear father

When that day comes
When that day comes
Will you leave with me
Will you leave?

You stoked fires in hell just to see her
You've got the sweetest demeanour
Why go breaking the legs of her ex-friends and lovers?
You're leading the exodus south
One word and we're all getting out
Go gather your things and significant others

564

TEAR ME APART

It's a hell of a long ways up
From the bottom to the top
You've had personal experience
Handling deliverance
Come on, come on
Why don't we talk about that?
Why don't we talk about it?

I know that it's absurd
But I hear you've got a way with words
Help me see my way clear
Accompany me out of here
Come on, come on
Why don't we talk about that?
Why don't we talk about it?

You're the echo in the chamber of my heart
I had wrestled with oblivion 'til she let me in
You weren't part of the equation but I've got to laugh
Deconstruct me from within
And when you feel those violent earthquakes start
Come on
Tear me apart
Tear me apart
I don't know where I'll end or where you'll start
Tear me apart

Now you may not be
All I've set you up to be
Yes I've made my share of mistakes
Can't I get an even break
What do you think?
Why can't we talk about that?
Come on let's talk about it

I have walked the world blind
Maybe I still do time to time
I was schooled to believe
If you give I shall receive
What do you say?
Why can't we talk about that?
Come on let's talk about it

You're the echo in the chamber of my heart
I had wrestled with oblivion 'til she let me in
You weren't part of the equation
But I've got to laugh
Deconstruct me from within
And when you feel those
Violent earthquakes start
Come on, come on
Tear me apart
Tear me apart
Come on, come on
I don't know where I'll end
Don't care where you start
Tear me apart

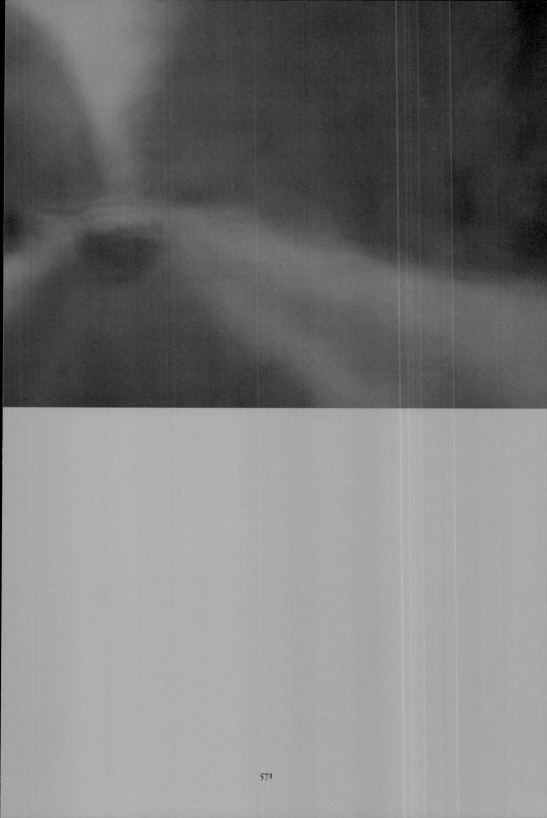

BEAUTIFUL COUNTRY

Her mind slept well
At high altitudes
All the way through Boulder
With the stupas pointing skywards
Like true believers
In crystal blue

The last of empire
December late
Such a sweet decay
And we drive all night
'Cause empires live long this way
Yes, we drive all night
Sleep by day

It's a beautiful country
What a beautiful country

Joy grows from her fingers
Her native hands
Long roots burrow down
Into her stomach spilling the air out of her lungs
It's the sharp end of the joyful life
You fell upon

The petals white
Veins are blue
She's filled with wonder
At the life within her
And the sight of you
At her own translucent heart
And the sight of you

It's a beautiful country
What a beautiful country

She's been playing her games
She's Billy the Kid
Changing the voice I'd been calling out with
We're losing our weight
Growing up thin
She stole the face of the lord so I won't recognise him
But it's all good, yes it's ok
We wouldn't have it any other way
Made our bed gonna lie in it
Watch the suns go down on the horizon

Way up in the pink hills
They'd drained the pool
There were sand flies buzzing
And the desert sun split us in two

It was an inland sea
Bombay beach
We were near narcoleptic
And the fireworks died with their heads down in the sand
This your land and soon your land will be my land too

It's a beautiful country
What a beautiful country

She's been playing her games
To keep herself hid
Changing the voice I'd been calling out with
We're losing our weight
Growing up thin
She stole the face of the Lord now I won't recognise him
But it's all alright, yes it's ok
We wouldn't have it any other way
Made our bed gonna lie in it
Watch the suns go down on the horizon
We're setting up camp far from it all
Where the dirt roads rise behind the strip mall
Remove ourselves we got nothing to give
Between the earth and stars
We'll find a place to live

Dust bowl diving
We ride the curves
She's railroad happy
And the longest trains hammer through
With their headlights blazing for you

It's a beautiful country
What a beautiful country

when we return you won't recognise us

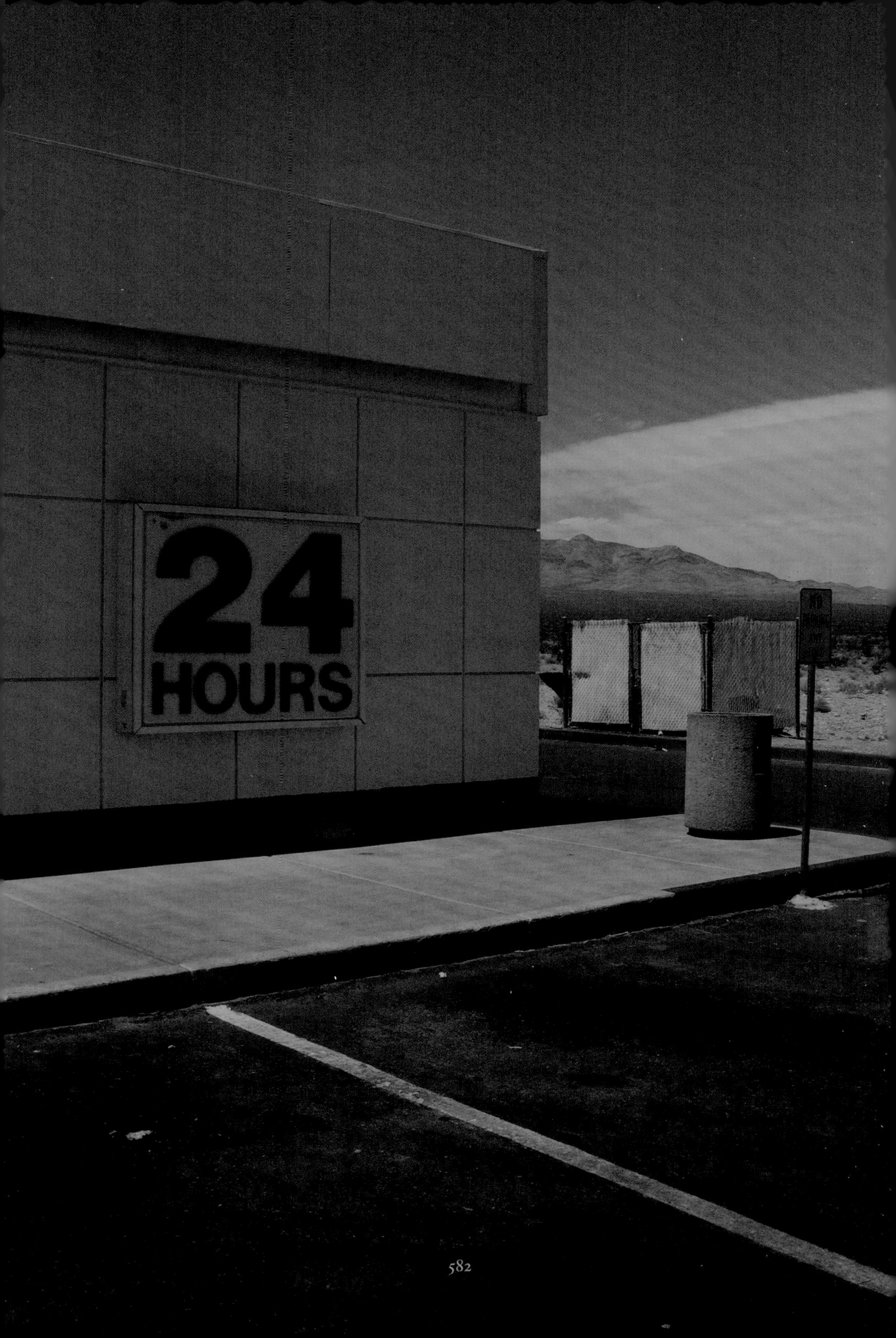
24
HOURS

WHERE'S YOUR GRAVITY?

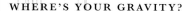

Baby's putting on her make up
Her mouth is swollen as a rose
Countdown, she wraps her legs around him
Weightless, she's taking off her clothes

Candy colours in her pocket
Bright children hiding in their rooms
Soft toys spread across her pillows
Self-annihilation couldn't come too soon

Where's your gravity?
Where's your mind?
Share your thoughts with me
Waste my time

Slow down, nothing's gonna save you
Ice cream dripping from your spoon
Ah but come now, you're always telling stories
Barefoot walking on the moon

Wake up and someone's bound to tell you
Your pretty face has gone to hell
So find them something you can trade with
Hand-make something you can sell

Where's your gravity?
Where's your mind?
Share your thoughts with me
Waste my time

(for kristamas klousch)

NORTH ALFRED ST.

I STOOD AT THE FRONT DOOR
COMPELLED, COULDN'T BREATHE
NOT THAT SHE'D KNOWN FOR CERTAIN THE CAUSE
BUT ISN'T IT ALWAYS PERSONAL BETWEEN TWO?
GOING OUT. WHERE? OUT
A TACIT ACKNOWLEDGEMENT OF WOUNDED DISAPPOINTMENT
DESPITE EVERY LENGTH TAKEN TO AVOID THE INEVITABLE
WHETHER I WISHED TO OR NOT AND FOR REASONS I DIDN'T UNDERSTAND
I WAS EXACTING PUNISHMENT
AND SHE THE ONE WHOM WE ADORE

WALKING, THE SUN WAS HOTTER THAN EXPECTED
MY ARMS COVERED, I UNZIPPED THE JACKET
LET A LIGHT BREEZE HAVE ITS WAY
DEEP SHADOWS ON UNEVEN CONCRETE, MANICURED LAWNS
AND SHRUBBERY WHICH EXPLODED INTO DAZZLING COLOUR
OR, NO MATCH FOR A WANING CALIFORNIA SUN
SMALL WHITE FLOWERINGS SHYLY LET THEIR PRESENCE GO UNNOTICED
AS I HIT THE MAIN BOULEVARD A YOUNG WOMAN
WITH A GORGEOUS FIGURE, BLUE DRESS, HEELED BOOTS
AND A LIGHT SHEER SWEATER TIED AT HER ELEGANTLY SLIM WAIST
CROSSED MY PATH
ON HER LEFT ARM A TATTOO THAT, AS I DREW CLOSER
HER HEAD TURNED TO WEIGH ME,
I NOTICED WAS A SMALL TREE WITH PATCHES OF CRIMSON
WHICH CONTRASTED WITH THE WARMTH OF HER BROWN SKIN
SHE EXUDED POWER, STRENGTH, AND AN EASY BEAUTY
SEEMED DRESSED FOR A FIRST DATE, A LATE AFTERNOON ENCOUNTER
THE TATTOO REMINDED ME OF MY ELDEST'S DRAWING OF A BROKEN TREE
ICE STORM OR THUNDER DAMAGED
WHICH BROUGHT ME BACK TO WHERE I'D BEEN ALL ALONG
STARING INTO THE EYES OF THE BELOVED CHILD ASKING MYSELF
WHY WAS I REMOVING MYSELF FROM HER SWEET COMPANY?
AND THE ANSWER ROSE LIKE THE MIST OF WATER FROM THE GARDENER'S HOSE
AS HE DAMPENED GRASS AND CONCRETE; JUDGMENT
HER UNBLINKING GAZE
THE DEGREES TO WHICH I MUST FALL SHORT OF EXPECTATIONS
THE HURT AND YES, AGAIN, THE DISAPPOINTMENT
MUST IT FOREVER BE SO FOR THOSE I LOVE? IN WHICH CASE
I'LL TAKE MY WALK ALONE, SLIP UNDETECTED LIKE A SUICIDE FROM A LANDING
ALL THE WHILE ACKNOWLEDGING THAT, YES
OF COURSE SHE'S RIGHT TO DEMAND THAT I ASPIRE HIGHER

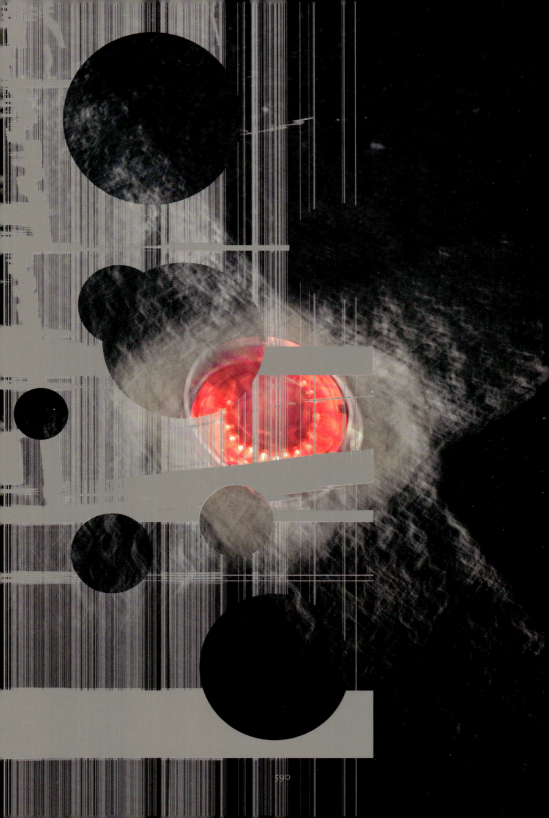

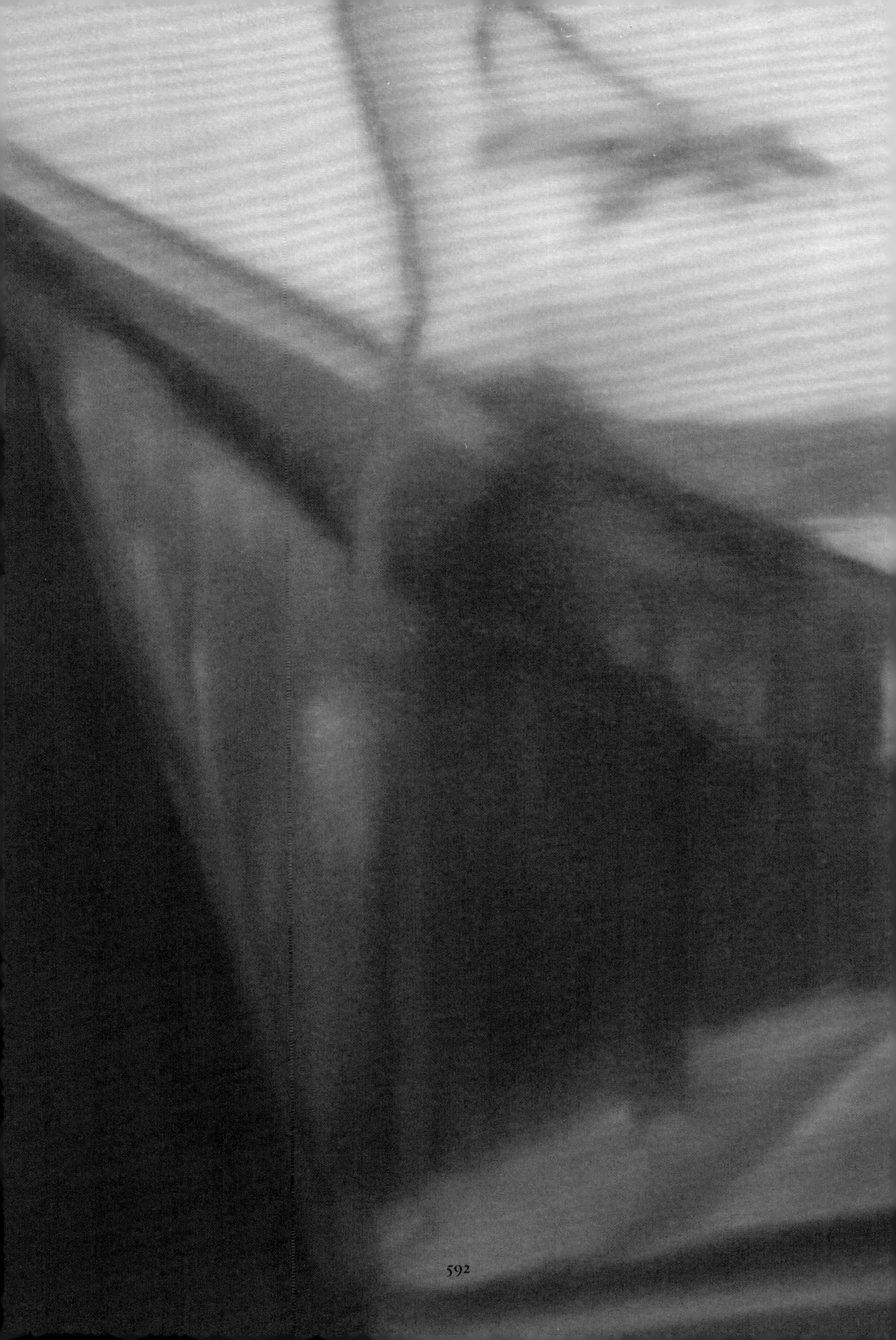

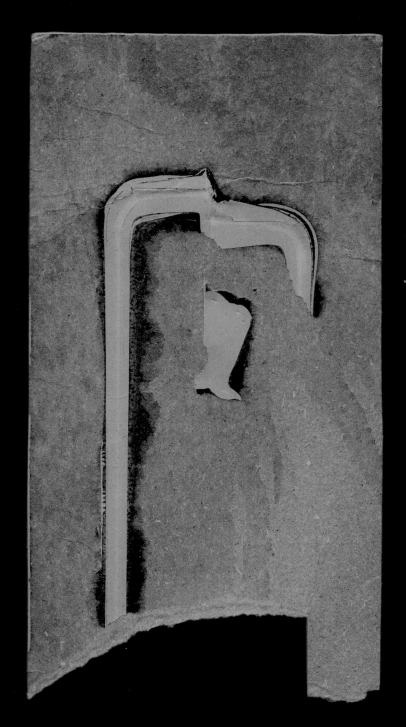

594

YOU TRIED TO CURSE ME LAST NIGHT

I PISSED IN MY SLEEP
ON RISING MY BACK MOVED OUT OF ALIGNMENT
THE ROOM ROILED FROM A BRUTAL BEATING
RECOILING IN AFTERSHOCK DANCING ON QUEER STREET
AS I FAILED TO FIND MY FOOTING

I STAND ON THE VERTIGINOUS EDGE OF YOUR SORROW
YOU FROM WHOM NO LIFE CAN GROW
ALREADY CORPSE, WHAT PUPPETRY ANIMATES YOU?
YOUR VOIDED SELF CONSUMED MY LIFE FORCE FOR THE LAST TIME
FIND ANOTHER DONOR FROM WHICH TO DRAW LIGHT
SWEET WOMAN, BEREFT OF INSIGHT, CONSUMED BY DOUBT
YOU MAY BE HARMLESS, BENEVOLENT EVEN
BUT THE SPIRITS THAT CLING TO YOU ARE RAVENOUS

NOTHING IS HAPPENING EVERYWHERE

I'd woken in a garden
Where metal crawls
The shoulders of dividing walls

I'd woken in a garden
Where metal divides
Almighty and small

So I'll never know you

All dunces are frightening
When fists are flying
They're terrifying

So I'll never know you

I'll dig but I'll never find you

And nothing is happening everywhere
So I'll never know you

I've run across cities
In which you've permission to cower
Relinquish your hold
On the vestiges of power

I'll dig but I will not find you
I'll dig

No desire for relevance
To say nothing of meaning
What a pitiful, pitiful feeling

Your efforts are futile
When did we become so very brutal?
I'll dig

I'd woken in a garden

And nothing is happening everywhere
So I'll never find you

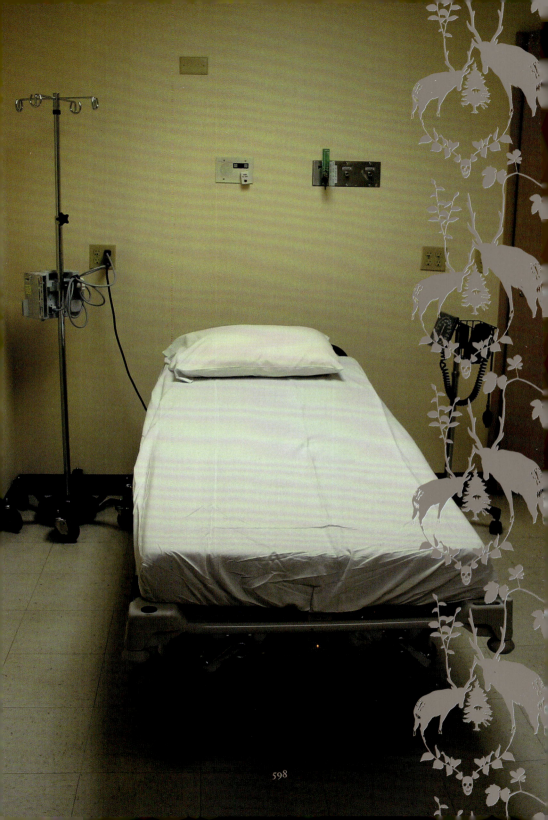

MODERN INTERIOR

And just because we stand in place
And just because we tow the line
Our hands still shake the dream awake
And just because we stand in place

We still feel extremely well
We still feel extremely well
And we still feel extremely well
We won't show so you can't tell
And we still feel extremely well

And this is what we sacrificed
Last one to leave turn out the lights

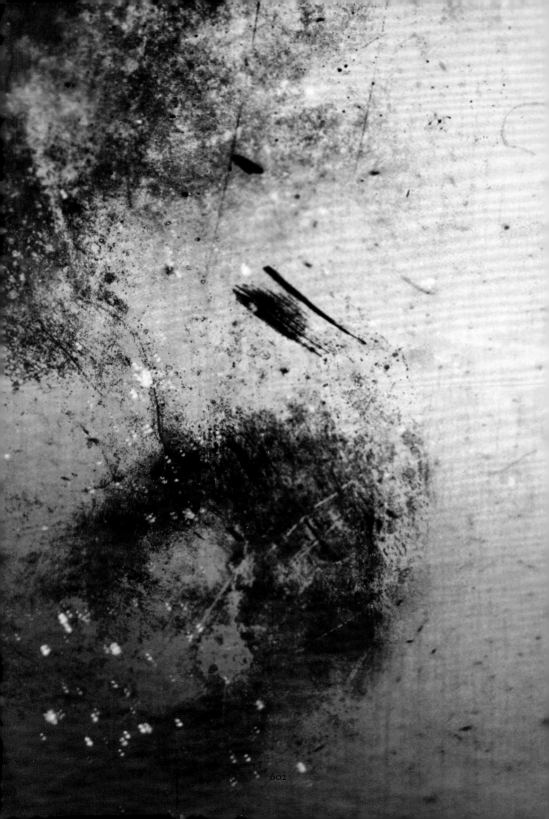

WANDERMÜNDE

saffron laudanum

velvet revolution

trauma ward

the farther away I am (minus 30 degrees)

dark pastoral

telegraphed mistakes

deceleration

DO YOU KNOW ME NOW?

And if you think you knew me then
You don't know me now
As the ground rose up to meet me
I kissed your mouth
You wore your boredom like an armour
But I turned you out
And if that brought us to our knees
We laughed all the way down
I prised my daddy's ring from my hand
And I made a bride
We grew a flower in the desert
We grew terrified
We were one, not one and the same
Something was lost somehow
And if you think you knew me then
You don't know me now

The planets high above you
Spun in houses of their own
You were dropped and hit
The ground running
But they failed to lead you home

And if you think you knew me then
Do you know me now?
I drew a child inside a womb
Justified myself
I stole the face of joy
The perfume of wealth
I atomised the boy within
Before he cut himself
You found the blood upon my clothes
And you washed it out
And if you think you knew me then
You don't know me now

There were children in the classroom
Erected without a nail
There were hornets in the heads of cattle
That vibrated to the sound

You cried wolf
I tracked one down and let it in
There were lambs, sure there was blood
There were psalms to sing
You could just see the bone jut out
Penetrate the skin
Did it dispel beyond all doubt the mess we're in?
You raised your head
I stared you down
You still don't know how
And if you think you knew me then
You don't know me now

I was happy, satiated
I was satisfied

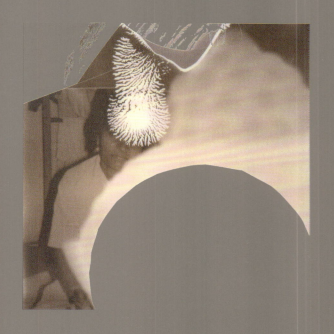

...nce Vought (Dallas) guided missile being launched from ground with aid of rocket-assist boosters.

February 1958

Mon	Tue	Wed	Thu
Full Moon 4th Last Quarter 10th	New Moon 18th First Quarter 26th		
3	4	5	6
10	11	12 ABRAHAM LINCOLN BORN 1809	13

612

ON LEAVING AMERICA

THE SUN IS WANING ON THE FAR SIDE OF YELLOWED NET CURTAINS
PARTED SO AS TO BEAR WITNESS TO THE JOURNEY
OF THE MODEST PASSENGER BOAT AS IT SPEEDS
BUSINESS MEN AND TOURISTS ALIKE ACROSS BLUE BAY WATERS
TOWARDS THE METROPOLIS

WE DISPOSED OF ONE ANOTHER LONG AGO
WITH STRINGS ATTACHED
WASN'T IT JUST A LITTLE CAVALIER THIS JETTISONING
OF ALL THAT WAS GOOD?
OR HAD THAT LONG CEASED TO BE THE CASE,
THE GOOD

THE SMALL CRAFT REACHES THE FARTHER SHORE SAFELY TIME AND AGAIN
IN WAYS WE WERE INCAPABLE OF DOING
WE'D FALL APART IN THE SHALLOWS TIRED AND DESPERATE
LIFEBUOYS HAULED US ASHORE TO MAKE ANOTHER GO OF IT
BUT OH THE ADVENTURES, THE FURTHER POSSIBILITIES
ALWAYS SEEMED ENDLESS UNTIL THEY DID NOT
LIKE NOAH, WE CAME TO GROUND ON A MOUNTAIN AND SET ABOUT
MORTALLY WOUNDING THE BODY OF LOVE
WELL, IF WE'RE HONEST, IT WAS ALREADY WELL SCARRED
BUT THERE WAS NO GETTING OVER THIS SACRIFICE
ON THE ALTAR OF SAINT PETER AND THE LOST SOULS OF THE SEA
WHY DOES THE PULL OF FAMILY TUG AT THE HEART
SO MANY YEARS AFTER THE FACT
EVEN NOW

THESE STRINGS, IMPOSSIBLY FRAIL WOOLLEN THREADS,
SUSPEND THE LAST OF THE LIFEBOATS
BONE SHATTERING BEAKS OF SEABIRDS CIRCLE IN READINESS
NEW PATTERNS WILL FORM FROM OLD, WE KNOW THAT
ARE YOU, LIKE ME, STILL UNPREPARED FOR THE FALL?

an exchange between

DAVID SYLVIAN

and

MARCUS BOON

"How much can you take away and still have a song?" This is the only note I have left on what was supposed to be a list of questions for David Sylvian. It reminds me of the beautiful moment in Leonard Cohen's "Tower of Song" where "I said to Hank Williams/How lonely does it get/Hank Williams hasn't answered me yet/but I hear him…" I didn't ask David "how lonely does it get?", but he answered me anyway, if you read between the lines, and carry on reading, or better still, listening…
– *Marcus Boon*

— **MB:** I just listened to "Manafon". I wish I'd listened to it a week ago because I've been sort of at my wit's end, and the first track on the disc in particular spoke to something I've been feeling rather intensely without being able to articulate it, or knowing anyone else who was able to do so. As with "Blemish" and some of your other recordings, I'm very thankful to have that experience of something obscure reflected back to me in a way that I am able to recognise.

— **DS:** Can't ask for more than that really.

— **MB:** I've been thinking a lot about "deflation" recently, and the bubble not only in the financial markets, but in values, practices, activities, ideas in general. And the sense that all of these bubbles are bursting or deflating. I think it's true in music, and the turn you took with "Blemish" is a rare thoughtful response to this problem… that melody, song, noise etc. themselves have become sites of a bubble that makes it almost impossible to listen to them, since all one hears is their "importance", their value as capital, as gesture in a marketplace saturated with gestures. If "Manafon" reminds me of anything it's

Cage's "Indeterminacy", another beautiful meditation on the question of form...

— **DS:** Oddly, the subject of "indeterminacy" has come up a lot lately both related to this and current work. I'm also familiar with the Cage work of that title and fascinated, as many composers over the years have been, by what can be done some place between overly determined composition and its opposite and how to bring the two closer together. Not exactly a new problem but relatively new to the area of songwriting, at least in this context. After all, all writing is an act of improvisation on some level. And the emphasis here is in the compositional process rather than the notion of repeat performance. That old chestnut of the fixity of the recorded performance... .

— **MB:** It's very low-key, but moving too. If there's a danger, it's in your voice, where I can feel the temptation to sing "beautifully" (this being one of your gifts), and the further temptation to refuse that gift by speech-singing or extreme lack of affectation. It lends the disk a strange sense of drama though, since in the end so much depends on very small decisions about intonation. And in the end this is part of the music's power, that sense of struggle at the level of your voice.

— **DS:** Of course these decisions are core for most singers in any context but they do become magnified under such circumstances. Some might feel there's an estrangement between singer and context which is part of the work's attraction for me. In some instances there'd be little difference in taking a field recording of say, sounds in a cafeteria, isolating 6 minutes and approaching this as a workable context for vocal composition... and indeed, that's how some of these ideas came together for me.

— **MB:** I don't imagine this was an easy disk to make, and the time right now makes it almost impossible to move forward, but you've found a way, and that's really something.

— **DS:** In terms of responding to the material to hand it wasn't a difficult album to make. The difficulties came in finding the raw material I was looking for. You don't walk into a roomful of free improvisers and say "this is what I want you to do". At least I didn't. The skill is in choosing the right constellation of players for each set up and then gently nudging the session in the direction you feel might prove the more fruitful. With each session I had some vague parameters that helped me locate what it was I was after (and at the later sessions we had the benefit of listening to some of the earlier for guidance). In every session some amazing material surfaced but it wasn't always of the kind that best served my interests or allowed room for the voice. Bit like hunting I guess... sitting patiently, waiting for the right species to show itself. Fascinating really.

— **MB:** So how did you go about the hunting here? Are you writing the songs in response to the improvisations?

— **DS:** I am, as road tested on the Derek Bailey tracks on "Blemish". It comes down to making the right choices regarding who to work with in what constellation. If you get that combination right something is bound to come out of the sessions that'll be close to anticipated... as far as that is possible. Gentle nudging, guidance, shifting of focus, pairing off performers, taking this one out of the picture, adding this... it's a fascinating way of digging for a particular kind of gold. The first sessions in Vienna lasted for eight days. I started with Polwechsel, Franz Hautzinger and Fennesz, later came Noël Akchoté (didn't make it onto the final album), then Keith Rowe joined us. Most of the material used came from the last two days with Keith, Christian (Fennesz), and Michael Moser and Werner Dafeldecker of Polwechsel. It took time for me to find what it was I was looking for but once the right combination was hit upon I knew I'd unearthed this, for want of a better term, modern chamber music I was after. Tokyo was a one day session. There was greater clarity and sense of purpose as a result of the time constraint but by that time I also had a clearer idea what it was I was after and how to find it. The only real specification made prior to the session was that Otomo Yoshihide use turntables with vinyl that featured chamber or modern string quartet music of some sort. The final session in London was also a one day affair. Again, I felt confident that I could find what I needed in that time frame with this incredible line up. I'd previously been given a session of improvised piano by John Tilbury which I'd managed to "track" into the earlier sessions but this was the first time we worked together in person. Philipp Wachsmann was also a part of the London line up but again, didn't make the final cut.

— **MB:** But I still don't understand how the recordings relate to the sessions, whether you're using them as material and then dubbing vocals after editing and structuring in Pro-Tools... or are you literally improvising the song during the improv session and the recording is the same as the session? Or...?

— **DS:** I take the sessions and work on them at a later time. I attempt to "improvise" lyrics and melodies as I go, writing and recording all in a matter of hours. The basic tracks themselves undergo little or no editing as such. The structure pretty much remains as given from the original sessions. I might add an introduction or overdub other elements onto the original take. Here's a couple of examples: "Senseless Violence": Recorded in Vienna with Rowe/Polwechsel/Fennesz. I added guitar parts then layered Tilbury's piano into the track then added the vocal and an introduction. "Greatest Living Englishman": Initial take suggested acoustic guitar overdubs which I requested of Otomo and Tetuzi on the spot. I later cut and pasted some interesting turntable activity from an alternate take onto this track. I also added an introduction by cutting and pasting elements from an earlier take. Tilbury was added to the coda. Melody and vocal added. "Rabbit Skinner": no editing. Added acoustic guitar myself then vocals.

— **MB:** Why the title "Manafon"? I google it and I get a Welsh village... I know "why?" is always a bad question... .

— **DS:** "The question... why 'Manafon'" leads me on a journey that reveals something of the nature of the entire project. This is a good thing for me because I had to back off from the work, spend some time away from it, as I'd begun to lose perspective. If someone had asked the seemingly simple question; "So, what's this album about?" I'm not sure I'd have had a ready answer. If we start with the track "Manafon" we're looking at a description of a man, a man of faith, who struggles with that faith, who imposes an order on the external world in the hope of finding it internally. A man who embraces the morals and values of his faith and lives by them but who also struggles with the silence that burns inside his own heart and mind. God's silence. He's a man out of time who begins to look, on the surface, more like some tragicomic figure as time passes. While he seems to be an insufferable individual in many ways there's a quixotic element in his quest for knowledge, for upholding morals and values that even he struggles with when it comes to believing in their efficacy. Each verse is a description of minor aspects of the life of the poet R.S. Thomas. The last two lines that end the piece are my own commentary. It spells out the sense of disillusionment and disorientation that the album starts with in "Small Metal Gods". Therein lies one of the central themes behind the album. The title "Manafon" alludes to another. Manafon is indeed a village in Wales,

a village in which Thomas lived for some time and served as Rector to the parish.
In this small village Thomas had trouble filling the pews of a Sunday but in a sense
it was something of an idyllic spot in which to raise a child (he was a strict, taciturn and
somewhat indifferent parent), master his profession and write his poetry. So the
physically real village became for me a metaphor for the poetic imagination. A resource
that's called upon to unearth meaning, lend comprehension, provide motivation, a
source of inspiration. It often plays a similar role in life for some as faith does for many.
I came to feel that, in a sense, Thomas' faith in, and need of, his outlet through poetry
was more important than the faith that inspired it. They were uniquely, it seemed to
me, bound to one another. Not as in the religious poetry of his and other faiths which
generally speak of the ecstasy. He writes of the working poor and the landscape but
it's an austere world with little hope of comfort and so, by contrast, we are encouraged
to concentrate on the fate of our souls etc. (yes, he wrote his own sermons too).
But, alongside a kind of negation of many facets of his modern world (although, he
was an odd mix of the recluse and the public figure even going so far as to lead CND
marches and was very outspoken in favour of the bombing of English-owned holiday
homes in Wales), there's also this underlying doubt and struggle with his belief, an
uncertainty of the existence of the other (religious devotees are warned that this is
a most dangerous period in their evolution, a time of suicides and renunciations).
I wasn't sure I wanted to put a name, a source to the title track because my
interpretation of Thomas' life and work might be more a product of my own projections
rather than detailing the facts of his life and work although, as I said, the particulars
described in the piece are real enough. A man who exhorted Welsh poets to write in
their own tongue when this was something he was unable to do. (He did write an
autobiography in Welsh but it's my understanding that his poetry was exclusively
written in English as this was his mother tongue.) He moved further and further west
throughout his life until it was possible to move no further within the country he
believed should be independent. But these facts are of only passing importance.
As a source Thomas might only be of importance to me. The ambiguity of the lyric
might work in its favour?
— **MB:** Did you ever meet Thomas?
— **DS:** No... I'm not sure I would've wished to at the time although I'd be very curious at
this stage in life.
— **MB:** Why does his story resonate for you now?
— **DS:** I've read Thomas since the 1980s. There was something about his austere vision of
the world which, as I said, belonged to another time. He was of the generation that lived
through World Wars I and II, that rejected the easy comforts of modern life, that in a
sense wanted more to be asked of them by society and in turn wanted society to rise out
of its weak minded ambivalence and desires for basic pleasures and aim for higher goals,
a more noble sense of itself and its destiny. Thomas seemed in search of a deeper, more
profound connection with the natural and spiritual world whilst appearing to battle
against inner demons which show familiar signs of being born of repression. Very British
in that respect. What interests me is how individuals, in pursuit of "truth", to fulfill
a life's promise by living it with a sense of dignity and purpose, can find themselves
derailed, disillusioned. I'm not saying that's what happened to Thomas but I can't help
feel that his wasn't a happy existence or that the life he chose to live didn't bear

significant fruit or at least that which didn't have a slightly bitter aftertaste. He appears to have been profoundly single minded, inflexible, proud, disparaging. All qualities we think of today as standing in the way of our development. But there's still a part of me that applauds the effort, the adherence to a path, a devotion to a life's cause. For all its apparent bitterness and tragicomic contradictions there's something beautiful about the man's dogged devotion to writing, to poetry. Like the character in Tarkovsky's "The Sacrifice" who everyday waters the dead tree in the belief that one day it'll return to life. This is the work of faith isn't it? Thomas' path was complicated by the seeming expression of doubt in God's existence although when asked the answer was a matter of fact "of course I believe in God". Who or what we choose to believe in or deny is very telling isn't it? Maybe I'm attracted to the stories of individuals who search for meaning on their own terms. I'm increasingly wary of hierarchies and societal norms and traditions... of "givens'. But what I'm fascinated by is the devotion to a creative discipline. The meaning with which the work imbues the life regardless of its reception and, to a certain extent, its importance.

— **MB:** "Manafon" is a dark record, and the music often evokes a feeling of fear, a kind of creepy post 9/11 feeling, unsettled in a very quiet way—but the singing is a counterpoint to this, facing it, telling a story that passes through the zone of fear, responds to it...

— **DS:** There are many subtle and not so subtle references to the creative imagination throughout the album. Allusions, quotations etc. Each piece seems to deal with the twin subject matter of inspiration/imagination and disillusionment in its own way. "Random Acts..." looks at what it means to be disillusioned with the ways and means with which societal values are protected and defended and a possible scenario to come as the tightening strictures of law and order become too unreasonably repressive and spontaneous acts of terrorism, not based in ideology but in anger and frustration and the desire for a liberation from the overbearing guidelines of the state, erupt. Minor acts of destruction as a creative act. This is something that seems inevitable as reasoned argument, protest, and related acts become increasingly inhibited under law.

— **MB:** You've been one of the few singers, especially with "World Citizen", but also some of the tracks here, who's responded directly to the political situation in America and Europe after 9/11. I know a lot of people who think of you as a singer of "spiritual" or maybe existential songs about inner struggle are surprised at this. Where did the directness of your response to what's been going on come from?

— **DS:** Actually, I think there may've been more responses to 9/11 and the post-9/11 environment than may be apparent. Working with Ryuichi Sakamoto on a couple of projects that he instigated pushed me into writing overtly political pieces but I never felt very comfortable with this approach. The soapbox numbers which resulted leave little room for individual interpretation. It was interesting to touch upon that style of writing, a somewhat prosaic approach to lyric writing and if you're going to write an openly political piece for a specific cause there's no point in being the least bit indirect in your approach. But I tend to think of it as the antithesis of the kind of material that I'm personally interested in and a perversion of the innate power of music which has a potentially political element to it at all times, as to effect or stimulate change in one individual is a political act as far as I'm concerned. Having walked down that road on a couple of projects with Ryuichi I began writing material that appeared more grounded in current events or making references to contemporary events but in the context of

narrative, as reference, as possible catalyst. This was because there was no remit, I was
free to deal with the subject matter as I chose. The first piece that I felt happy with
in this respect was "Atom and Cell". It was written some time before "World Citizen
(I Won't be Disappointed)", which is a piece I'm also happy with, but released at a
later date. "Wonderful World" also deals with similar subject matter. Living in the
United States has also made me more politically aware because I feel there's so much
work to be done here in terms of equality, liberty, the raising of awareness on numerous
issues, the fight against the oppressive nature of the Christian right and the power of
multinational corporations, the lobbyists etc. The US, for all its eccentricity, is
powerfully conservative. I guess I tend to find that conservatism somewhat oppressive
and so certain issues have begun appearing in the work which mightn't be there
otherwise. Also, I have serious doubts that there's such a thing as a free press in the US.
More often than not the media seems to act as mouthpiece to the politicians mainly for
fear of losing access to them. The politicians certainly aren't thoroughly examined by the
media by any stretch of the imagination. Scrutiny of the Bush administration
pre- and post-war was almost wholly absent. All voices of dissent were suppressed or
eradicated which made it all the more important to add one's voice in the hope of
something, anything, breaking through.

— **MB:** It's striking how English things sound on "Manafon". Not just the lyrical concerns,
but even your own intonation and the choice of phrases... .

— **DS:** There was a desire to create a work that had a definitively British or, possibly
more specifically, English quality about it. Even with many nationalities involved in
its making that's something I hope I've managed to maintain in the finished work.
Why take that route? Most of the decisions made in this respect are initially of an
intuitive nature. An intuitive understanding of the nature of the work which presents
itself during the gestation period prior to conception and realisation. It's a map
against which every step taken on the road to realisation is measured and quantified.
It helps when making very elementary decisions about the nature of the work such as
the instrumentation (what is or isn't excluded e.g. no percussion) as well as the overall
tone, feel, and real content of the compositions. "Blemish" also wore its Englishness on
its sleeve (think of pieces such as "The Only Daughter" with lines such as "do us a favour,
your one and only warning, please be gone by morning"), in that sense and many others
"Manafon" is a companion piece. Maybe this "Britishness" is a product of trying to speak
with a true voice? To give voice to something that exists within me as memory, lived
experience, or knowledge. To place its roots in specific soil... and I'm not speaking of
musical roots which are something I've always fought against in a way, but in a specificity
bought about through circumstances of birth, in my case, London from the late 1950s
(write of what you know). To find voices to give voice to that experience. I found it
easier to write in the third person in that respect. Project my own concerns onto these
characters. I guess it's a bit like living in the States and reflecting on that British
character once removed. Distance helps. It allows you to speak some home truths via
sleight of hand. But there's absolutely no nostalgia in this examination of character.
It's a self examination and by extension an examination of certain aspects of the British
character and human nature in general although, I have to say, I'm not really an "everyman"
in that respect and maybe that's one reason why my work's failed to find a bigger audience.
Hard for me to tell. I only know what it's like to have lived inside my own skin.

— **MB:** To me something that resonates in the record is an odd sense of disillusionment with spiritual paths. I'm not sure whether "disillusion" is the right sense for it, but just scepticism about the community, the motives, the shiny images of deities that I know were made in a sweat-shop in Mumbai... to the point where I wonder what's left aside from something transcendental, that I have very strong feelings for and a deep attraction to, but which I've now subtracted all human links to, because I can't believe in the links any more. In a way, the "path" becomes truly open, but often I don't see any path at all. So maybe the whole universe becomes "improv" at that point?

— **DS:** This is an interesting development though isn't it? I've read, as I'm sure you have, that some teachers have recommended a thorough detox via professional analysis before ever approaching a path or discipline. I'm not sure that's a cure all but it's pretty difficult for us to see past our own deficiencies, our neuroses, and so see what clearly motivates us in our search. No doubt there's something primal in us that sets us on one journey or another but that's coloured or tempered by all manner of other needs and desires and it's here that we possibly come undone, use a distorting lens to enable us to see what it is we wish to see? It does become increasingly difficult to believe in the testimony of others... the links and lineage... there's so much self delusion, politics, power grabbing and maintenance etc. Once you've been through the wringer a few times, more than a few times, you begin to only believe in the voice inside yourself which rings true*. Personal experience before you've time to (re)interpret it... epiphanies, unanticipated, sustaining. I find the whole process fraught with difficulty but fascinating. Letting go of ambition seems to be part of the process too. Ambition for personal progress. Yes, improv or winging it. I like the state of hopelessness. Hope really does tend to get in the way. It takes you out of the present towards an ideal. To live without hope but without a loss of love for life... that's a great starting place it seems to me.

* I don't believe in magic,
  I don't believe in I-ching,
  I don't believe in bible,
  I don't believe in tarot,
  I don't believe in Hitler,
  I don't believe in Jesus,
  I don't believe in Kennedy,
  I don't believe in Buddha,
  I don't believe in mantra,
  I don't believe in Gita,
  I don't believe in yoga,
  I don't believe in kings,
  I don't believe in Elvis,
  I don't believe in Zimmerman,
  I don't believe in Beatles,
  I just believe in me,
  Yoko and me,
  And that's reality.

God. John Lennon

(or alternately... delusion... all of it... and there's relief in that).

And there is no maker
just inexhaustible indifference
and there's comfort in that
so you feel unafraid

Snow White in Appalachia. David Sylvian

THE LAST OF THE SUN ALIGHTS ON PASSING
PLANES GLINTING IN A BLUE SKY SHELLED
BY CLUSTERS OF ATOMIC CLOUD, PLUMES OF
MUSHROOM GREY AND INNER ILLUMINATED
WHITE. TOMORROW I'LL BE LIT BY THAT SAME
SUN IN THE SMALL METAL GOD OF ALL THAT'S
TRANSITORY. A JOURNEY WESTWARD TOWARDS
A DARKENING PAST AND A BLOSSOMING FUTURE
BURGEONING WITH POSSIBILITY. THE RAYS CATCH
THE CROWNS OF INDECENTLY ABUNDANT TREES
TORMENTEDLY THRASHED THIS WAY AND THAT,
UNDERWATER PLANT LIFE AT THE MERCY OF A
RIVER'S VIOLENT EBB AND FLOW. TINY INSECTS
ARISE FROM THE DEEP. WHY DO THEY FLY AT THIS
ALTITUDE I WONDER. WHAT NEED OR THERMAL
UPLIFT BRINGS THEM TO MY WINDOW? IN THE
DISTANCE THE CIRCUMNAVIGATION OF THE VOID
BY AN INCREASING NUMBER OF BIRDS. WHAT
SPECIES IS THIS? HOW OFTEN HAVE I WATCHED
THEM RISE IN THE DUSK'S DARKENING, HIGHER
AND HIGHER, AN ASCENSION INDIFFERENT TO
BEAUTY, A GATHERING INTUITIVE THOUGHT,
A PRAYER. MAJESTIC. A ROYALTY'S SUBJECTS
ENACT A DEVOTIONAL HYMN. HIGHER AND HIGHER
THEY CLIMB UNTIL THEY ENTER THE DUSK CLOUDS,
AN UNEARTHLY EARTHBOUND VAULT OF HEAVEN.
I WILL RISE WITH THEM WHEN I GO. WHEN I GO
MAY I RISE WITH THEM. WHEN I GO, AM GONE. RISE.

art direction, book concept & editorial guidance: DAVID SYLVIAN
book design & calligraphy: CHRIS BIGG

PHOTOGRAPHY, PAINTING & DRAWING CREDITS

pg's. **2 & 3** *painting:* ATSUHIDE ITO
pg. **5** *photography:* DAVID SYLVIAN
pg's. **6 & 7** *photography:* NIGEL GRIERSON
pg. **11** *painting:* ATSUSHI FUKUI
pg. **12** *painting:* KATHARINA GROSSE
pg. **41** *drawing:* TORU KAMIYA
pg. **47** *photography:* ERIC RONDEPIERRE
pg. **51** *drawing:* TACITA DEAN
pg. **56** *photography:* DAVID SYLVIAN *drawing:* HANNAH BERTRAM
pg. **59** *photography:* YUKA FUJII
pg. **61** *photography:* DAVID SYLVIAN
pg. **62** *photography:* YUKA FUJII
pg's. **64 & 65** *photography:* KRISTAMAS KLOUSCH
pg's. **66 & 67** *photography:* NORIKO TANAKA *drawing:* TORU KAMIYA
pg's. **68 & 69** *photography:* YUKA FUJII
pg's. **76 & 77** *original album sleeve treatments:* CHRIS BIGG *pin-hole image:* DAN JAY
pg's. **78 & 79** *drawing:* TACITA DEAN
pg. **80** *photography:* YUKA FUJII
pg's. **84 & 85** *photography:* CECIL BEATON
pg's. **88 & 89** *photography:* YUKA FUJII
pg's. **90 & 91** *photography:* YUKA FUJII *drawing:* DAVID SYLVIAN
pg's. **92 & 93** *photography:* DAVID SYLVIAN
pg. **96** *photography:* YUKA FUJII
pg's. **98 & 99** *photography:* YUKA FUJII
pg's. **100 & 101** *painting:* ATSUHIDE ITO
pg's. **102 & 103** *photography:* YUKA FUJII
pg's. **104 & 105** *photography:* SHINYA FUJIWARA
pg's. **108 & 109** *photography:* MASATAKA NAKANO
pg's. **114 & 115** *original album sleeve treatments:* CHRIS BIGG *pin-hole image:* DAN JAY
pg's. **116 & 117** *drawing:* TORU KAMIYA
pg's. **119 & 120** *painting, drawing:* ATSUSHI FUKUI
pg's. **122 & 123** *photography:* DAVID SYLVIAN
pg. **124** *drawing:* DENISE SCHATZ *overlay treatment:* CHRIS BIGG
pg's. **126** *drawing:* HANNAH BERTRAM
pg's. **130 & 131** *painting:* ATSUHIDE ITO
pg. **132** *photography:* YUKA FUJII
pg. **135** *painting:* ATSUHIDE ITO
pg. **136** *photography:* DAVID SYLVIAN
pg. **137** *photography:* YUKA FUJII
pg. **138** *original photography:* UNKNOWN *treatment photograph:* DAVID SYLVIAN
pg. **141** *drawing:* ATSUSHI FUKUI *overlay treatment:* CHRIS BIGG
pg's. **144 & 145** *photography:* NIGEL GRIERSON
pg's. **148 & 149** *original album sleeve treatments:* CHRIS BIGG *pin-hole image:* DAN JAY
pg's. **151** *drawing:* HANNAH BERTRAM
pg. **152** *photography:* DAVID SYLVIAN
pg. **153** *photography:* NIGEL GRIERSON
pg. **155** *photography:* DAVID SYLVIAN *overlay treatment:* CHRIS BIGG
pg's. **156 & 157** *drawing:* TACITA DEAN
pg's. **158 & 159** *photography:* DAVID SYLVIAN *painting detail:* MARIKO SUGANO
pg's. **160 & 161** *painting 'The Childish Game":* MARIKO SUGANO
pg. **163** *painting "Dream of a Poet":* MARIKO SUGANO
pg. **164** *photography:* DAVID SYLVIAN

I'm indebted to the artists whose work has contributed to this volume. thank you dearly.

love/gratitude to those that have stayed with me on the journey:

BERNARD AND SHEILA BATT
STEVE AND GOBI JANSEN
RICHARD CHADWICK
NEIL WARNOCK
YUKA FUJII
ADRIAN MOLLOY
CHRIS BIGG
ADAM PHILLIPS

AMEERA-DAYA & ISOBEL ANANDA SYLVIAN

and to the many musicians, artists, writers, composers it's been my good fortune to
have worked with and, in some instances, to have known.

The iniquity of oblivion blindly scatters
her poppyseed and when wretchedness falls
upon us one summer's day like snow, all
we wish for is to be forgotten.

W.G. Sebald

(The Rings Of Saturn)